# THE PARABLES OF THE GOSPELS

## AND THEIR MEANING FOR TODAY

### HUGH MARTIN, M.A.

THE ABINGDON PRESS

NEW YORK      CINCINNATI      CHICAGO

MARTIN
THE PARABLES OF THE GOSPELS

Copyright, 1937, by
HUGH MARTIN

Printed in the United States of America

# CONTENTS

# CONTENTS

6 CONTENTS

# PREFACE

WHEN this book was well on its way, there appeared two very important contributions to the study of the parables. Professor C. H. Dodd's *The Parables of the Kingdom* was issued when this book was half written, and Doctor Oesterley's *The Gospel Parables* when it was still further advanced. During the process of revision I was happily able to make use of them, and I owe much to them though I have not always been able to accept their conclusions. I warmly commend them to those who wish to study the subject more thoroughly.

These books show a ripe scholarship which is entirely out of my reach, but their scope and purpose is so different from that of my more humble effort that I hope there may still be room for it. My purpose has been to prepare an exposition which would be of service to teachers in classroom and pulpit, as well as to those who wish to study the parables for their personal interest and profit. Many of the previous books of this kind which have been of great service in the past are now somewhat out of date. They miss the help of more recent New Testament scholarship and they are written in a different language and against a different mental and social background from ours. To the professional student some of them will long be of value, but the ordinary reader does not find it very easy to get from them what he wants.

My object has been to discover the original meaning of the parables, and then to apply its message to the lives of men and women in our modern world. I have tried to take advantage of the work of scholars, and my main debts are, I hope, adequately acknowledged in the text. But it did not seem fitting to burden a popular book with a great apparatus of notes and references.

I have based my chapters, for the convenience of the ordinary reader, on the Authorized Version. The use of a good modern translation is, however, a very great help and is a commentary in itself. I am grateful to Messrs. Hodder and Stoughton for their kindness in allowing me to print Doctor Moffatt's version in this book. I would urge those of my readers who do not already possess it to secure the whole of his *New Testament,* as I feel sure they will wish to do after reading his rendering of the parables.

I should like to express my gratitude to my friend the Rev. Edward Shillito, who read the typescript and made some valuable suggestions; to Miss Eileen Nikolin, who grappled with the original manuscript; and to Miss Margaret Holloway, who has read the proofs.

### NOTE

The version of the parables printed at the head of the chapters is that of *The New Testament: A New Translation,* by James Moffatt, and is included by special permission of the owners of the copyright, Messrs. Hodder and Stoughton.

# THE PARABLES OF THE GOSPELS

## I

## INTRODUCTION

STORYTELLING was Jesus' favorite method of teaching. If we knew nothing about Him except that He was the author of the parables of the Gospels, we should be compelled to number Him among the greatest. If they were by any other, we should speak of the literary genius they betray. They are among the greatest short stories in the world. It is only because Jesus Christ is incomparably above such praise that it seems almost incongruous to think of them thus. How vividly they present a character in a few words, with that "economy of material" that is the mark of a great artist! They are unique in literature. Lord Tennyson's son tells of a conversation about the parables between his father and Robert Browning. "Perfection beyond compare," Tennyson called them, and Browning fully agreed.[1]

In *Concerning the Ministry*[2] Doctor Oman refers to an attempt made to improve the parables by a gentleman called Harwood, writing in 1768. He found them too plain for his taste. He rewrote

[1] *Memoir of Lord Tennyson*, I, p. 325.
[2] Page 124.

the parable of the prodigal son, and began: "A
gentleman of a splendid and opulent fortune had
two sons." He rendered thus the reflections of
the prodigal in the far country: "I am determined
to go to my dear aged parent, and try to excite
his tenderness and compassion for me. I will kneel
before him and accost him in these penitent and
pathetic terms—'Best of parents! I acknowledge
myself an ungrateful creature to heaven and to you!
. . . Condescend to hire me into your family in the
capacity of the meanest slave.' " We return with
relief from such pomposity to the matchless sim-
plicity and power of the original.

The parables are ancient and Eastern, and that
is part of their fascination. They take us into
another world. We watch the sower striding along
the furrows beside the Galilean lake; we listen to
a poor widow begging for justice from an unscrupulous judge; we see an Eastern wedding in
progress or the guests assembling for a feast. We
observe the snobbish, self-satisfied Pharisee march
up the Temple steps and the shrinking publican
at a distance. We watch the women baking bread
or sweeping the house, the shepherd and the fisher-
man at work. We see the crash of the badly
built house as the flooded river swirls about its
walls.

But these tales are modern too, because they are
really about men and women, and men and women
have changed little since Jesus spoke. "How like
so and so!" we think. Sometimes, it may be, with
something of a shock, we have to say, "How like
me!" He knew what was in man. Jealousy and

greed, pride and penitence, love and hate still abide. Boys still visit the far country and find its dainties turned to husks. Rich fools—and poor ones too—still think that money is all that matters. Men and nations still fall among thieves.

Yes, and still the Sower sows the seed of the Word in human hearts. Some are so hardened and superficial that they do not take it in. Some are so worried or so keen on having a good time that the seed never gets a chance. Some are full of enthusiasm and make ardent Christians for a few weeks, but give it up when it gets difficult. But there are some who have ears to hear, who receive the Word into their hearts. They know life's real worth, and theirs is the joy of the harvest,

If we start reading the parables as literature, we are unlikely to end there, for these stories of Jesus are spirit and life.

## Why Did Jesus Teach in Parables?

Perhaps our Lord chose this method of teaching partly because He loved telling stories. He was, as we say, "a born storyteller," and perhaps first practiced the art before a fascinated youthful audience in the home at Nazareth.

But we must remember also that Jesus found this method in use. The parables are not so unique a form of religious teaching as the ordinary modern Bible reader is apt to imagine. There are, of course, parables in the Old Testament, for example, 2 Samuel 12. 1-14; 14. 1ff.; 1 Kings 20. 38-43; Isaiah 5. 1-7; Ezekiel 17. 1-10; 19. 2-9, 10-14;

20. 45-49. But it was also a common method of religious teaching in the time of our Lord. Many parables are to be found in rabbinical literature covering the period 300 B. C. to 200 A. D. It was characteristic of Jewish teachers to convey truth imaginatively rather than in abstract argument. There were many familiar themes which were manipulated and applied in varying ways; the king who says or does something, the scene of a feast or a field or a vineyard. Doctor Oesterley, who has made a special study of this subject, gives many examples of rabbinical parables in *The Gospel Parables in the Light of Their Jewish Background*. His comment will be felt to be just by those who have any acquaintance with them. "Interesting and instructive as [the parables of the rabbis] often are, they stand on an altogether lower plane [from the Gospel parables]. It is not prejudice that prompts us to say this—far from that, we have a warm feeling of sympathy with a great deal of the rabbinical teaching; but we are convinced that any impartial reader of the two sets of parables, the Gospel and the rabbinical, will be forced to admit that the latter compare very unfavorably with the former."[3]

Jesus, then, did not invent the parabolic method. He found it in use in His day. But He made of it something new. One is reminded of what Wordsworth wrote of the sonnet when Milton took it up—

> "In his hand
> The Thing became a trumpet; whence he blew
> Soul animating strains—alas, too few!"

[3] *Op. cit.*, p. 11.

But, of course, we must look more deeply. Our
Lord would not have taken up this method had
it not commended itself to Him. Jesus used the
parabolic method, and loved to use it, because the
realm of nature from which He drew His stories
was to Him a sacrament of things divine. To His
seeing eye it spoke of its Maker and His ways.

Wordsworth writes in *The Excursion*[4] of the
child who picks up a shell and putting it to his
ear thinks he hears the murmuring of the sea—

> "Even such a shell the universe itself
> Is to the ear of Faith; and there are times
> I doubt not, when to you it doth impart
> Authentic tidings of invisible things."

That is true to the thought of Jesus. We can well
believe that the words attributed to Him in the
Oxyrynchus Papyri are indeed from His lips.
"Jesus saith: Ye ask who are those who draw us
to the Kingdom if the Kingdom is in heaven? The
fowls of the air and all the beasts that are under
the earth or upon the earth, and the fishes of the
sea, these are they which draw you, and the Kingdom of heaven is within you, and whosoever shall
know himself shall find it."

The spiritual world and the natural are both
products of the same Mind and purpose. Nature
without and human nature within illumine each
other, and both in spite of sin point to the God
who made them. Human fatherhood is the best
clue we have to the Power behind the universe
(compare Luke 11. 13). This invisible world, as the

---

[4] Book IV, "Despondency Corrected."

apostle Paul says, is designed to make known the
invisible things of God (Romans 1. 20).[5]

"Jesus of Nazareth taught men to see the operation of God in the regular and normal—in the
rising of the sun, in the falling of the rain, the
growth of the seed into the plant.  If men had
been ready to follow Him in this, much of the
actual conflict between religion and science would
have been avoided."[6]  He does not look only for
divine "intervention" in the abnormal and unusual.  The beauty and order of providential care
revealed in nature tell us something about God.

"We are not asked," writes Professor Manson,
in his outstanding book on *The Teaching of
Jesus*,[7] "to argue from the intricacy of the machin-
ery to the ingenuity of its inventor.  The whole
emphasis is on the personal relation of the Creator
to His creatures.  God clothes the lilies of the field
and God feeds the birds, one might almost say,
because God is fond of beautiful flowers and fond
of birds. . . . The picture of God making
clothes for the flowers and preparing meals for the
sparrows is the picture of a God who is Lord of
creation by being the servant in love of all His
creatures.  The statement, 'He that would be chief
among you must be the servant of all,' has its
application even in the heavenly places.  There,

---

[5] Compare Milton, *Paradise Lost*, V, 1, 575:

> "What if earth
> Be but the shadow of heaven, and things therein
> Each to other like, more than on earth is thought!"

[6] Temple, *Nature, Man and God*, p. 46.
[7] Page 163.

indeed, it has its deepest meaning and its perfect realization."

The parables are not moral anecdotes attached to the sermons to illustrate spiritual truth and make it more palatable. They are accurate pictures of the life of nature or the habits of men—or if they are, as sometimes, startlingly inaccurate, the very point of the picture is its inaccuracy. It is by their truth to nature that the parables reveal truth about the spiritual world.

Jesus leads men to learn about the unfamiliar world of the spirit from what they may see around them in the familiar world of home and field. The parables are the fruit of a wide observation and love of nature and of men. He had that seeing eye and hearing ear which He bade us to have, and in the parables He is saying to us "Look!" He does not argue, rather He helps us to see.

How much He saw! He bids us look at sunrise and sunset, the ways of wind and weather, the habits of the fig-tree, the vine, the thornbush, the thistle, or the mustard plant. The humble scarlet anemone that carpets Galilee in the springtime as the daisies carpet our English meadows, was to Him more splendid than a king in royal robes. He saw the weeds in the wheatfields and the reeds waving in the wind. He was familiar with the ways of the eagle and the dove and the raven. He watched the hen gathering her chickens under her wing, the fledgling sparrow falling from the nest. He has an eye for the sheep, the ass, the dog, the camel, the wolf, the swine, the serpent, the scorpion, the moth. His kindly but searching

glance falls too upon the life of men around Him.
He knew His own trades of carpentry and house-
building, and something of fishing, the casting of
nets and the signs that tell when a shoal is about,
and the cares of the shepherd and the farmer.
He has illustrations from home life that will appeal
especially to the women on the edge of His
audiences, on the patching of old clothes and the
baking of bread.   He watches children at their
play and observes the ways of courts and counting-
houses.   He is painting life, the real life of rich
and poor, of rogues and philanthropists, and there
is much in the picture that is due to His sheer
interest in the theme and has no bearing on the
moral.

Such an outlook upon nature seems to have
been unusual in His day, and, indeed, there are
few speakers or writers in any day with so concrete
and living a manner of speech, so colored by
the events and surroundings of everyday life.
Because of His fidelity to fact the parables, says
Professor Dodd, have "unique value as historical
documents.   It may safely be said that the literature of the Roman Empire contains no other such
vivid pictures of the life of the common men under
its rule."[8]

All this knowledge and insight He turned to
use in the revealing of God to men.   We might
say, therefore, that Jesus used the parable method
because it was the clearest and most forceful way
of bringing home His message.

---

[8] *The Authority of the Bible,* p. 148.

The answer would seem obvious, were it not
for certain verses in the Gospels which are bound
to cause perplexity. In Mark's Gospel (4. 10ff.),
when the Twelve asked Him for an explanation
of the parable of the sower, Jesus is reported as
saying: "Unto you is given the mystery of the
kingdom of God: but unto them that are without,
all things are done in parables;[9] that seeing they
may see and not perceive, and that hearing they
may hear and not understand, lest haply they
should turn again and it should be forgiven them."
This looks as though Jesus were saying that the
purpose of His use of parables was to *prevent*
people from understanding His message. It is
impossible that Jesus should have meant this,
because it is out of harmony with all His life and
teaching. His mission was to bring men to repentance, not keep them from it.

In Matthew (13. 13-15) the words are reported
differently. "Therefore speak I to them in
parables, *because* seeing they see not, and hearing
they hear not." That is, because these people are
so slow to understand spiritual truth I speak to
them in stories to give them the best chance of
understanding. This is very different from Mark's
apparent suggestion that it was the intention of
Jesus that people should not understand.

But we shall perhaps understand Mark's real
meaning if we remember that he is reporting a
quotation by our Lord from Isaiah (6. 9-10), given

[9] Literally, "all things happen to them in parables," which
means, I think, that they understand the story but not its inner
meaning.

more fully by Matthew, in which the prophet
ironically says that all his best efforts to teach his
fellows end in such failure that it almost looks as
if that were the very purpose of his teaching. The
more he taught them, the more they misunder-
stood. Isaiah is speaking somewhat bitterly of the
disappointing result of his mission, and does not
mean that it was really his intention. So, perhaps,
if Jesus used the words in the form found in Mark
—though Matthew's version seems more natural—
He too was speaking ironically and not literally.

Doctor Oesterley[10] points out that the Septuagint
version of Isaiah (6. 19), instead of "Make fat
the heart of this people," reads, "For the heart
of this people has become gross." This makes
clear what is probably the intention of the Hebrew.
The Hebrew sounds as if the prophet were to be
the cause of making the people renegade. In the
Septuagint it is the obstinacy of the people which
is the cause of their falling away; the words of
the prophet simply serve to reveal the real state of
their hearts.

The repeated appeals of Jesus to listen and
understand make it clear, if the point needs any
demonstration, that He spoke in order to bring
home truth to men's minds and hearts. (See, for
example, Matthew 18. 12; Mark 4. 9; 7. 14.) Certainly, we know from the Gospels that some of
the parables made their point felt immediately.
Often the story held the hearers for its own sake,
and it was not till the end that they understood

---

[10] *Op. cit.*, p. 52.

its bearing upon themselves.   Especially vivid is
the ending of the story of the vineyard (Luke 20.
15-16), "What therefore will the lord of the vineyard do unto them?   He will come and destroy
these husbandmen and will give the vineyard unto
others.   And when they heard it, they said, God
forbid."   *They* understood.

And while there are depths in these stories
which the wisest of men cannot plumb, who could
fail to understand the message of some of them?
Truth so embodied in a tale can surely enter in
at lowly doors.   The lengthiest exposition of the
meaning of pardon could not be so clear and
moving as that picture of the father running to
meet his erring son with a welcoming love that
asks no questions, content with the all-sufficient
fact that he has come home.

Some people, doubtless, could listen to any
story without appreciating its meaning.   To careless and superficial minds any parable might
remain a tale.   Spiritual things are spiritually
discerned.   Yet may it not be said that even for
the careless and superficial there could be no better
way of teaching?   The story, remembered as a
story, sticks in the mind.   By and by the meaning
emerges as experience quickens the understanding.

This is not to say that the lesson of the parables
is obvious.   No one can study the commentators
without being amazed by the divergent meanings
that scholars can draw out of the same verses.
Part of the trouble is due to Western ignorance of
the Oriental setting.   More is often due to theological presuppositions which the parables must

be made to fit.   But most of the trouble is caused
by trying to be too clever and by insisting upon
treating all the parables as if they were allegories.
Yet even to the sincere and well-equipped modern
scholar there is much that is puzzling, and for all
of us the parables point the way over uncharted
seas.   The mind of Jesus is too great for us to
compass.

## WHAT IS A PARABLE?

So far we have been using the word "parable"
popularly, without any attempt at definition, but
it is impossible to go further without being more
precise.

It may well seem curious to the uninitiated
reader to find that there is great difficulty in defin-
ing the nature of a parable, or even in deciding
which are "the parables of the Gospels." Some
would include in the list every simile, metaphor, or
proverbial expression used or quoted by our Lord,
such as "Physician, heal thyself," or the warning
to put new wine into new wineskins.   Since few
speakers have been so pictorial in their language
as He, a very long list can be so compiled. Others
are as strict in excluding whatever does not accord
with their definition, and even the stories of the
good Samaritan, the Pharisee and the publican,
and the sheep and the goats are ruled out by
some scholars as "not parables."   Thus the number
given by various authorities varies from seventy-
nine to thirty-three.   Professor Manson reckons
sixty-five.[11]

---

[11] *Op. cit.*, pp. 66-69.

Clearly, therefore, it is not very easy to decide
what a parable is.  By its Greek derivation the
word means the act of placing one thing beside
another for the purpose of comparison—a definition
which would cover the widest range.  The corresponding Hebrew word (*mashal*) is used in the
Old Testament to include simile, allegory, proverb,
paradox, and riddle.  In the Synoptic Gospels the
word *parabole* is applied to twenty passages includ-
ing the proverb quoted above (Luke 4. 23), and
other similar uses (for example, Luke 4. 39), paradox (Mark 7. 17), similitude (Mark 4. 30), allegory
(Matthew 13. 18), and illustrative instance (Luke
12. 16).  Many classifications of all the parables
under such headings have been attempted.  But,
like the numerous systems of classification by subject matter, these all seem unsatisfactory and rather
forced, without contributing much to their appreciation.

More than mere verbal issues are, however,
involved in the much-debated question as to
whether our Lord ever used allegory.  An allegory
is a narrative in which every character and every
progressive development in the story figuratively
represents something else.  *The Pilgrim's Progress*
is the best-known allegory.  Every event in that
story and every feature of the landscape is intended
to have its parallel in the experience of the Christian soul in its pilgrimage "from this world to that
which is to come."  Paul's description of the
soldier's armor is an allegory of the Christian's
equipment—the belt of truth, the shield of faith,
the helmet of salvation, and so forth (Ephesians 6.

14-18).  If the parables are allegories, we shall be
entitled, and, indeed, obliged, to look for spiritual
counterparts for everything.  In the parable of the
good Samaritan, for example, we shall identify
not only the hero of the story and the victim, but
also the ass, the inn, the innkeeper, the wine, the
oil, and the two pennies. Tertullian explained
that in the parable of the prodigal son, the father
represents God, the father's wealth was the knowledge of God one has by nature, the citizen to
whom the prodigal attached himself was the devil,
the swine are demons, the best robe is the position
from which Adam fell, and the welcome feast is
the Lord's Supper. Until quite recently most
volumes on the parables were full of such interpretations.

It is beyond question that the allegorical method
of interpretation has led in the past to ridiculous
results.  But past extravagances need not lead us
to deny that Jesus ever used allegory, as a number
of modern scholars have done.  That there is an
allegorical element in some of the parables seems
beyond serious doubt.  It is not disputed that if
we accept the interpretations ascribed to Jesus in
the Gospels, the parables of the sower, the wicked
husbandmen and the tares are allegories.  That
we cannot be sure of having in every case the very
words of our Lord is clear on any basis of argument; the fact that the different evangelists record
the same parables differently prevents us from
advancing any such claim.  There is also good
reason to see in some of the parables traces of
modification in the light of later events.  But it

is not therefore necessary to dismiss as entirely
unjustified the interpretations affixed to the three
parables mentioned. A more detailed discussion
will be found under each parable.

In general, however, those scholars are right
who warn us against allegorical interpretations.
Such methods only obscure. In the mass of detail
you forget that the story of the good Samaritan
was told in answer to the question "Who is my
neighbor?" and that its purpose is to tell us that
the neighbor we are to love is any man of any
race who needs our help. The details are just part
of the setting on that Jericho road which the
hearers knew so well, with its bandits, its travelers
and its inn—a road up which Jesus had just
traveled when He told the tale. It is being
ridiculous to seek for spiritual meanings for the
two pennies, and to assert, for example, that they
represent the two sacraments. They are there,
rather, to show that the Samaritan intended to
finish the job properly, and there were two because
two were needed to pay the bill.

Certainly, we shall go far astray if we forget that
the parables were all spoken to a living group of
hearers with a meaning for them, first and foremost.
What would have been meaningless to that audience cannot belong to the heart of the interpretation. "If Jerusalem represents the state of primal
innocence and the descent to Jericho the fall of
man, if the robbers are sin, the priest and the
Levite the moral and ceremonial law, the good
Samaritan Jesus; if the inn is the Church, the innkeeper church officials, and the two pence the

two sacraments, then to the people who first heard the parable it meant nothing at all."[12]   With later Christian experience and fuller knowledge of the life and teaching of Jesus, later generations may see more deeply into His meaning than His immediate audience, but the central point of the parable could not be something necessarily unintelligible to them.

## HOW ARE THE PARABLES TO BE INTERPRETED?

While no rigid rules can be laid down as to interpretation, some guiding principles can be indicated.

(a) *The Context.*—It follows from the principle already formulated that the parable must have been intelligible to its hearers, that the key to its meaning should be sought in its original setting.   If we knew the context in which the parable was first spoken, the occasion that called it forth, the audience to which it was addressed, we should have an invaluable clue to the lesson our Lord intended to teach.   It illuminates the story of the prodigal son to know that it was spoken in the face of the sneers of Pharisees, and that its object was to justify Jesus in his associating with publicans and sinners; so with the settings of the stories of the good Samaritan and the unmerciful servant.

Of course it is possible that the parable is not in its right setting in the Gospels as we have them now.   Matthew sometimes gives the same parable

---

[12] M'Fadyen, *The Message of the Parables*, p. 45.

in a different setting from that provided by Luke,
and we cannot be sure which of them is right.
Certainly, we cannot assume that the parables
which Matthew groups together in his thirteenth
chapter were all part of one discourse, as he seems
to suggest.  Nor were the parables of the lost coin,
the lost sheep, and the lost son grouped together
by Luke (15), necessarily told at one time, though
the unity of their thought is clear.  Still less can we
rely upon any chronological connection with the
parables in chapter 16, introduced by the non-
committal phrase "and he said also unto the disciples."  Very rarely can we be sure of the historical setting, though we may at least infer that the
position assigned to it is a clear indication of what
the evangelist confidently believed the parable to
mean.

Nevertheless, there are not a few cases where
parable and context seem wedded together and
each naturally illustrates the other.  It is the
occasion which makes clear, for example, why the
elder brother appears in the story of the prodigal
son, which might otherwise have ended with the
prodigal's return.

Recent New Testament scholarship maintains
that the materials of the Gospels were transmitted
orally in self-contained blocks, which were later
pieced together by the evangelists.  The "Form-
Criticism" school insist that the Gospel setting
is more often provided by the situation in the
early Church at the time of the completion of
the Gospels than by the original "setting in life."
The Church tended, not unnaturally, to read the

sayings of our Lord in the light of their own urgent needs.[13]

In its extreme form this theory is not convincing, and it is hard to see why much of the framework also might not have been transmitted. The original setting might have been transmitted with the parable from the first. While allowing for editorial modification we need not be eager to question the authenticity of the setting recorded in the Gospels themselves. Each case must be taken on its merits.

Certainly, the recognition, demanded by the facts that some of the parables have varied in transmission or even have been deliberately modified to point a moral of importance to the early Christian communities, does not mean that we need have serious doubts about their authenticity. As Professor Dodd says, "They have upon them, taken as a whole, the stamp of a highly individual mind, in spite of the rehandling they have inevitably suffered in the course of transmission. Their appeal to the imagination fixed them in the memory, and gave them a secure place in the tradition. Certainly, there is no part of the Gospel record which has for the reader a clearer ring of authenticity."[14]

(b) *The Central Theme.*—Further, each parable has one main lesson, relevant to the situation in which it was spoken. The details generally belong

---

[13] For a valuable exposition and criticism of this school of thought, see Vincent Taylor, *The Formation of the Gospel Tradition.*
[14] *The Parables of the Kingdom,* p. 11.

to the scenery of the parable, as was urged above in connection with the story of the good Samaritan. In the hidden treasure and the pearl, to take another illustration, two stories are told to enforce the truth that to gain the supremely valuable possession no sacrifice is too great. Any likeness which may be traced or imagined between the kingdom of God and a pearl is accidental. So also it is irrelevant to discuss the propriety of the conduct of the man who found the treasure, or of the unjust steward; the point of the story lies elsewhere.

It is to misunderstand the spirit and method of our Lord's teaching to seek in each parable for a balanced presentation of the whole Gospel. Jesus does not balance and qualify: "on the one hand," "on the other hand." He speaks with emphasis the truth needed at the moment as if it were the only truth—"He that *hateth* not his father and his mother. . . ." A parable has in it one truth and not necessarily every truth.

I may, perhaps, quote in relation to the parables what I have written elsewhere about the moral teaching of our Lord. "Jesus was no legislator; rather, if we must draw such comparisons, He was a poet. The legislator codifies and defines and surrounds his laws with qualifications and provisos. The poet is suggestive, symbolical, illustrative, epigrammatic. He is not afraid of a sweeping assertion that for the moment forgets all qualifications. There is that kind of quality about the teaching of Jesus—a spontaneity of spirit, an individuality of response to a particular situation which is the very antithesis of the necessarily generalized and desiccated legal approach to human conduct."[15]

"The poet," writes Sir Philip Sidney, in his *Apologie for Poetrie,* "beginneth not with obscure definitions which must blur the margent with interpretations, and load the memory with doubt-fulness. But he cometh to you with words set in delightful proportion, . . . and with a tale he cometh forsooth unto you, with a tale which holdeth children from play, and old men from the chimney corner."

In short, we must search for the main theme of the parable, and press the details only in so far as they contribute to the exposition of that main theme. The problem of interpretation is to find, if we may, first, the occasion in which the parable originated; secondly, the central theme of the story; and then, thirdly, to relate the central theme of the parable to the needs of the original occasion. Only when that has been done can we safely apply the lesson to our own lives and circumstances.

"The parable elicits a judgment in one sphere in order to transfer it to another."[16] The hearer is led to a judgment in a sphere where he is un-biased in order to bring home to him the truth in a similar situation in which he is concerned. Two out of many possible illustrations are the

---

[15] *Morality on Trial,* p. 51. If C. F. Burney is right, Jesus was a poet in the strictest sense of the word, not only in the spirit of His teaching, but also in its form. See his book, *The Poetry of Our Lord.*

[16] A. T. Cadoux, *The Parables of Jesus,* p. 56.

story of the ewe lamb, told by Nathan to David
(2 Samuel 12. 1-14), and the story of the two debtors, which Jesus told to Simon the Pharisee (Luke
7. 36-50). Often the hearers of a parable do not
see where the tale is leading them until the climax
comes, and they find that they have pronounced
judgment on themselves.

(c) *The Teller of the Parable.*—The supreme
context of all the parables, if one may use the
expression, is the personality and mission of their
author. Emerson thought that historic Christianity
had "dwelt with noxious exaggeration about the
person of Christ."[17] Voices are regularly raised
bidding Christians to concentrate on the teaching
of Jesus and not to confuse the world with doctrines about Him. In fact, however, the teaching is
inextricably bound up with the personality of the
Teacher.

This principle involves, to begin with, that the
parables must be interpreted in harmony with the
teaching of Jesus, taken as a whole. We ought to
hesitate to build a Christian doctrine upon a
phrase or an incident in a parable, especially if it
seems to conflict with the general trend of our
Lord's teaching. This is no imaginary dilemma, as
will be seen in the study of several of the parables.

But the principle is even more far-reaching than
this. Jesus was no mere ethical teacher pro-
pounding moral lessons. He was, and knew that
He was, Christ, Messiah, Saviour. He had come
at the fullness of the times. It was an hour of

---

[17] *Address to Divinity Students.*

crisis—*the* hour of crisis in human history. He had come to cast fire upon the earth. Nothing could be the same afterward. History is either "Before Christ" or "in the year of our Lord." There are few of the parables that do not reveal the presence of the hour of destiny, and our Lord's consciousness that He had been "sent" to play a unique part in human history.

It is one of the many paradoxes in the life of Jesus that with this sense of crisis and urgency there goes a spirit of peace and leisure. Doctor Oman rightly protests against exaggeration here: "Schweitzer gives a picture of a short ministry of Jesus as one succession of excited expectations and enthusiastic endeavors. Sit down and read through the Gospel of Mark, on which he mainly relies, and you will find not only a man of peace, but a man of leisure. He never preached the gospel of peace in a flurry. All His teaching speaks of leisure, not only from itself and from the world, but even from His ministry. To teach in parables at all meant leisure. He noticed the flowers and the sky and the farmer at work and the children at play."[18]

Yet to say no more would be to misunderstand. "The gospel of peace" is not a complete description of the preaching of Jesus. We may set beside the words of Doctor Oman the equally true words of Professor Dodd, who speaks of "the volcanic energy of the meteoric career depicted in the Gospels. The teaching of Jesus is not the

---

[18] *Concerning the Ministry*, p. 34.

leisurely and patient exposition of a system by the founder of a school. It is related to a brief and tremendous crisis in which He is the principal figure, and which indeed His appearance brought about."[19]

## WHAT IS THE KINGDOM OF GOD?

This crisis is associated with the coming of the kingdom of God and His relationship to it. The Kingdom is at the very center of the teaching of Jesus, and many of the parables open with the phrase, "The kingdom of God is like . . ." If we are to understand our Lord's teaching in general or the parables in particular, we must try to answer the question, "What did Jesus mean by the kingdom of God?" This might seem to the uninitiated to be a fairly easy question. In fact, there is no more debatable or debated question in the whole range of New Testament scholarship. To discuss the issue fully would lead us beyond the scope of such a popular expository treatment of the parables as this seeks to be, and would involve an unduly lengthy discussion.[20]

Two points may be dealt with rapidly. The distinction which some writers have sought to draw between "the kingdom of God" and "the kingdom of heaven" is nonexistent. "Heaven" is

---

[19] *Op cit.*, pp. 25-26. Von Hügel calls attention to this combination in Jesus of calm and leisure with "intensity of expectation" in *Essays and Addresses on the Philosophy of Religion*, Vol. I, pp. 125ff.

[20] I have treated the subject more fully in *The Necessity of the Second Coming*. Modern scholarly surveys can be found in Dodd's *The Parables of the Kingdom;* T. W. Manson, *The Teaching of Jesus;* W. Manson, *Christ's View of the Kingdom of God.*

a frequent substitute for "God" in Jewish writings, and the substitution was made from motives of reverence and for no other reason. It may be well also to state, without here arguing the point, that it is impossible to identify the kingdom of God with the Christian Church.

The word "kingdom" is perhaps a little unfortunate as a translation for the Gospel word on account of its geographical suggestion—though, as a matter of fact, the same ambiguity exists in the Greek. To speak of the reign or rule or sovereignty of God would perhaps convey the thought more correctly. We shall also go astray if we think of the kingdom of God, as so much popular writing and speaking does today, as being a kind of Utopia, a future Golden Age. The fundamental idea in the Gospels is one of religious worship and obedience, not of social betterment; though, of course, if God ruled wholly in the hearts of men, a social transformation would inevitably follow as a consequence.

Manson well sums up the implication of the phrase thus: "Primarily the Kingdom is a personal relation between God as King and the individual as subject. Then it appears in the world as a society, something which might be called the People of God. This society consists of all those who are linked together by the fact of their common allegiance to one King."[21]

Jesus did not invent the phrase or the idea. To think of God as King has always been character-

---

[21] *Op. cit.*, p. 134.

istically Jewish. In the *Authorized Daily Prayer Book* of the United Hebrew Congregations of the British Empire in use today and based upon the traditions of many centuries perhaps the most characteristic phrase is "Blessed art thou, O Lord our God, King of the universe." In the time of Jesus popular thought about the kingdom of God had been shaped by two streams of influence—the prophetic and the apocalyptic. The prophets of the Old Testament often looked forward to the Day when God would intervene and usher in a new order of righteousness and peace and gladness. In some of the prophets the coming of the Day of the Lord was associated with a Messiah, an anointed servant of God, sometimes identified with a contemporary hero, sometimes pictured as a supernatural figure.

At the time of the great struggle for Jewish independence, under the Maccabees (168-135 B. C.), and the reaction after it, the new outlook of apocalyptic began to play its part.[22] The apocalyptic writings are spread over a period of three centuries, two before and one after the birth of Christ, and undoubtedly largely molded and expressed Jewish thought in the time of the Gospels. There are a large number of these books, with much the same outlook and using the same kind of highly symbolical language. There are two examples in the Bible, the books of Daniel and Revelation, and from them much can be learned about the literature in general.

---

[22] The word "apocalyptic" literally means "revelation," but the real content must be gathered from the description that follows.

The apocalyptic books have been described as "Tracts for Bad Times." They express faith triumphant over despair. There was no sign of the glorious future foretold by the prophets. God's people continued to be oppressed by arrogant foreign powers. Only a supernatural intervention of Almighty God could avail to deliver them. The present world order must perish altogether and a new heaven and a new earth be ushered in. The object of the apocalyptic writings was to hearten the oppressed by the assurance that God would so intervene. Behind the strange imagery they use is a magnificent faith that refused to believe that evil could have the last word.

In the time of Christ two main conceptions of the coming of the kingdom of God had emerged. (a) There was the belief in a warrior Messiah ruling from the throne of David over a kingdom established by military and political means. Much in the Old Testament lent color to this idea. This was probably the most popular view and had led to many unsuccessful risings against the tyrant. The kingdom of God had come to mean for many Jewish nationalism in face of a Roman oppressor. (b) But there was also prevalent the apocalyptic faith in a supernatural intervention of God Himself to do what human agency could not do. A quotation will illustrate this belief and incidentally provide a good example of apocalyptic literature. It is quoted from R. H. Charles's *Apocrypha and Pseudepigrapha* and comes from *The Assumption of Moses:*

"And then His Kingdom shall appear throughout all
    His Creation. . . .
For the Heavenly One will arise from His royal
    throne,
And He will go forth from His holy habitation,
With indignation and wrath on account of His
    sons, . . .
For the Most High will arise, the Eternal God alone,
And He will appear to punish the Gentiles,
And He will destroy all idols,
And thou, Israel, shalt be happy, . . .
And God will exalt thee."

With both streams of thought it may be said that
the main conception was that of God's authority *de
jure* becoming acknowledged and exercised *de facto*
over all men. Where they differed was in their
views as to ways and means. In general it may be
said that the prophetic outlook gives more place to
human response and co-operation than apocalyptic.

Jesus Himself recognized a divine revelation in
the Old Testament prophets and used their imagery. We must not read His poetical and symbolical words, with their Old Testament background,
as if they came from a modern Western textbook
of theology. Further, we must remember that the
minds of the disciples were colored by these
current conceptions which would inevitably affect
the form in which the teaching of Jesus would be
recorded. This process can be seen at work in
the Gospels, where accounts of what seems obviously to be the same saying may vary. Matthew
tends to heighten the apocalyptic emphasis.

Some scholars have maintained that our Lord
shared the current apocalyptic outlook completely

and thought of the kingdom of God as future and supernatural, and to be ushered in by a sudden catastrophe. But the Gospels can be made to fit such a view only by a wholesale cutting out of passages which have as good a claim to be considered authentic as those upon which such scholars rely. However the difficulty is to be met, the Gospels speak of the Kingdom both as a present living reality and also as something which is still to come.

(a) The kingdom of God is declared to have come with the coming of Jesus (Mark 1. 14-15). Something new and effective has happened which means that the power of God is manifested in the world as it was not before. In Jesus God is at grips with evil (Matthew 12. 28=Luke 11. 20; see also Matthew 11. 2-6=Luke 7. 19-23). Jesus does not, like John the Baptist, look forward to the coming of a greater. The disciples are to rejoice, for that which the prophets of old had longed to see is now before them (Matthew 13. 16-17=Luke 10. 23-24; compare Matthew 12. 41-42=Luke 11. 31-32). This seems also to be one implication of the puzzling saying in Matthew 11. 12-13 (=Luke 16. 16). Whatever else it means, it means that with the advent of John the Baptist the age of the law and the prophets came to an end; now are the days of the kingdom of God (compare Luke 4. 17-21).

To the challenge of this existing kingdom of God men are summoned to respond in penitence and obedience. The Kingdom is there in their midst and they are invited to enter it. But it is

there whether they enter it or not (compare Luke
10. 10-11 and 13. 34).

Jesus is not pointing merely to a happy future
when all men shall do the will of God. He is
calling men to live here and now a life of loyalty.
In the Lord's Prayer, the clause, "Thy will be
done on earth as it is in heaven," seems clearly to
be meant as a definition or explanation of the
phrase "thy kingdom come." To pray that prayer
truly it must first of all mean, as Manson points
out, "thy will be done by me."[23]

Jesus as Messiah institutes the Kingdom. It is
manifested in the world as others follow Him.
Behind many of the parables is the conviction that
the rejection of His message will bring personal
loss and national disaster. To decide not to enter
the Kingdom is to make "the great refusal," as
Dante called it. No sacrifice can be too great to
make to gain an entrance. No other loyalty can
be allowed to stand in the way (Mark 8. 34–9. 1=
Matthew 16. 24-28, Luke 9. 23-27; Mark 10. 21-31
=Matthew 19. 21-29, Luke 18. 22-30; Luke 14.
26, 29=Matthew 10. 37-38; Matthew 7. 33=Luke
12. 31).

It is of great interest to notice that the phrase
"eternal life" is used in Matthew's Gospel where
the parallel passage in Mark's Gospel speaks of the
kingdom of God (Matthew 18. 8-9=Mark 9. 43-47;
see also Mark 10. 17 and 23 and parallels). So the
Kingdom from one point of view is a kind of life
to be entered here and now. In the fourth Gospel

---

[23] *Op. cit.,* p. 161.

the place of the kingdom of God, so central in the Synoptic Gospels, is entirely taken by "eternal life." "Eternal" does not imply life in a future heaven, but a quality and condition of life to be received now as a lasting possession.

To enter the kingdom of God is to submit one's whole life to God's rule and to seek first the doing of His will. When the scribe said that to love God "with all the heart and with all the understanding and with all the strength, and to love his neighbor as himself, is much more than all whole burnt offerings and sacrifices," Jesus declared that he was "not far from the kingdom of God." He understood its secret.

The Kingdom has come. Jesus has fulfilled the hopes and prophecies of the past. Whoever will pay the price may enter here and now.

(b) But at the same time there are passages which imply that the kingdom of God is still in the future.

Jesus declares that many are to come from the east and the west to sit with the patriarchs and the prophets in the kingdom of God (Matthew 8. 11; Luke 13. 28-29). The parable of the mustard seed also pictures the growth of the Kingdom until the nations come into it.

When our Lord has His last meal with the disciples, He looks forward to a renewal of fellowship in His Father's kingdom (Matthew 26. 29; Mark 14. 28).

He says that many then present shall not die till they see the Kingdom coming in power (Mark 9. 1; Matthew 16. 28; Luke 9. 27). There are

several passages which speak of the coming of the
Son of man in power and glory, though we ought
not perhaps to identify the coming of the King-
dom with this (Matthew 26. 64=Mark 14. 62;
Mark 8. 38; Matthew 16. 27-28; Luke 9. 26-27;
Matthew 19. 28; Luke 22. 29-30).

The thirteenth chapter of Mark, with its parallels in Matthew 24 and Luke 21, takes us onto very
debatable ground. Their emphasis is upon the
future, but it is not necessary to call them in
evidence here.[24]

We can at least claim that there are numerous
passages in the Gospels which look forward to a
period of delay or growth, and to an eventual
dramatic climax to human history, sometimes
spoken of as the coming of the kingdom of God.

Professor Dodd holds that the future tenses are
symbolical of the eternal and timeless element in
the Kingdom. "So far as history can contain it,
it is embodied in the historic crisis which the
coming of Jesus brought about. But the spirit
of man, though dwelling in history, belongs to the
eternal order, and the full meaning of the Day of
the Son of Man or of the Kingdom of God he can
experience only in that eternal order. That which
cannot be experienced in history is symbolized by
the picture of a coming event."[25]

Any view put forward by Professor Dodd com-
mands respectful consideration, but it may be
doubted if this really does justice to all the evidence. I believe myself that the permanent spirit-

---

[24] See *The Necessity of the Second Coming*, pp. 38ff.
[25] *Op. cit.*, p. 108.

ual meaning of the doctrine of the Second Coming, with which the present discussion is intimately connected, is to be found in the belief in a final triumph of the cause of God *on the field of history*. Making all allowance for symbolism, it is to this that these Gospel passages, and others discussed in the volumes quoted, bear witness. Of course the Kingdom cannot fully come on earth, because that would limit it to the then living generation of men and women. It must come "in heaven" as well as on earth. But the Gospels maintain that the victory of God will be won in reality and on the same plane as that where the struggle is.

Let me try to sum up. There is no doubt as to the twofold element in our Lord's teaching about the Kingdom. The Kingdom is present and it is also to come. It is here in germ in historic reality. But it will come in fullness in the future, when the seed sown has come to harvest. There is no contradiction here. The two thoughts belong naturally together.

Questions as to the *time* of this consummation of the Kingdom I have discussed fully in the book to which I have referred. I believe our Lord was not greatly concerned with such questions. Almost the only definite statement He made about them was that He did not know the day and the hour (Mark 13. 32; Matthew 24. 36). But as He looked over history with the eyes of faith, He believed that the triumph of God's cause, the final and full coming of the Kingdom, was an absolute certainty. He foresaw a slow progress of youth, but He fore-

saw also swift achievement and dramatic event.
God would win His triumphs day by day as men
responded to the appeal of His love.

But one day there will be harvest. The king-
doms of this world shall become the kingdom of
our God and of His Christ.

### The Classification of the Parables

A large number of different schemes have been
formulated; indeed, almost everyone who has
written a book about the parables has grouped
them differently.

Any arrangement by subjects seems unsatisfactory. The groups inevitably overlap, and it is
not really possible to arrange the teaching of Jesus
as if He were a theological professor expounding
systematic theology.

Probably the best arrangement would be in
chronological sequence, if we could be sure of it.
So we might trace the development of the teaching
in response to the developing situation. While
conscious that no finality can be reached, I have
attempted to place the parables in this book in
the order in which they may have been spoken
in the ministry of Jesus. Any such arrangement
must obviously be very conjectural. I have, however, grouped together certain parables for convenience in exposition.

As already explained (page 21), it is hard to know
where to draw the line in selecting parables for
exposition. Many other brief parables and parabolic sayings have really as good a claim for inclu-
sion as, say, the parable of the empty house, but to

include everything would have meant a volume of alarming size. Certainly, all the larger and more familiar parables are treated here.

For convenience in reference I have retained the traditional titles even where, as explained in the comment, they are not really very adequate.

## II

## THE ROCK AND THE SAND

Now, everyone who listens to these words of mine
and acts upon them will be like a sensible man who
built his house on rock. The rain came down, the
floods rose, the winds blew and beat upon that house,
but it did not fall, for it was founded on rock. And
everyone who listens to these words of mine and does
not act upon them will be like a stupid man who built
his house on sand. The rain came down, the floods
rose, the winds blew and beat upon that house, and
down it fell—with a mighty crash.—*Matthew* 7. 24-27.

Why call me, "Lord, Lord!" and obey me not?
Everyone who comes to me and listens to my words
and acts upon them, I will show you whom he is like.
He is like a man engaged in building a house, who dug
deep down and laid his foundation on the rock; when
a flood came, the river dashed against that house but
could not shake it, for it had been well built. He who
has listened and has not obeyed is like a man who built
a house on the earth with no foundation; the river
dashed against it and it collapsed at once, and the ruin
of that house was great.—*Luke* 6. 46-49.

WINCHESTER CATHEDRAL, huge, low-
lying, massive, looks as solid and enduring
as the hills. But in 1905 serious signs of weakness
appeared in the fabric. Ominous cracks made it
clear that something was wrong. Some experts
suggested buttresses to prop up the walls, or tie-
rods to hold them together. But one insisted on
probing deeper. He sank deep shafts down to

43

the foundations and discovered that the great
cathedral had been built upon a bog. The original
builders had laid tree trunks flat on the soft,
watery soil, and on that had reared their building.
It was hardly surprising that trouble should arise
for their successors. The marvel was that the
building had stood so long. In the end a diver
had to be employed in a deep-sea diving suit to
dig down through eight feet of peat beneath the
old foundations and underpin them with concrete.[1]

Even a cathedral is no stronger than its foundations. And what is true of cathedrals and dwelling-
houses is equally true of human personalities.

There is perhaps nothing in the picture gallery
of the parables more vivid than the story of the
wise and the foolish builders which Matthew sets
at the close of the Sermon on the Mount—with
supreme fitness, whether this was, indeed, a sermon
delivered as a unity, or, as scholars now think, a
compilation of sayings on many occasions.

Two men set out to build houses. One came
upon the smooth sandy deposit of a flood. What
could be better! No need for troublesome level-
ing. So there, without bothering to dig a foundation, he built his house.[2] And no doubt it looked
very fine. The second man spent a great deal of

---

[1] The story is told in *Sixty-three Years of Engineering*, by Sir
Francis Fox, the civil engineer who devised the operation. The
diver was W. G. Walker. He worked for five and a half years in
water thick and brown from the peat, picking the peat out in
sections and replacing it by concrete.

[2] In Luke's Gospel one man digs a foundation; the other digs
none at all. In Matthew's Gospel the difference is in the choice
of the site; nothing is said about digging. See further *The
Realism of Jesus*, Findlay, p. 219.

time before he started on the actual job of erection,
in digging down through the sand and gravel till
he came to the solid rock. Then he began to
build. It took him a good deal longer than the
other man, and when he was finished, there was
not much to choose between the two houses so
far as appearance went.

But in due time the rainy season came. And
where the floods had been the floods came again.
"Torrential came the rain! Down swept the
floods! Angry roared the wind!"[3] The waters
ran down the ravine or "wady" in spate, like a
roaring tide, and swirled round the houses. They
gnawed at the sand on which the first house stood
and ate it away from beneath the walls. And the
house collapsed in crashing ruin. They raged
round the second house too, but beneath its walls
was solid rock and the floods raged in vain. The
house stood safe.

That is the difference, said Jesus, between the
man who does not obey My teaching and the man
who does. In following Me is stability and security.
In rejecting Me is disaster.

Even to those to whom Jesus is Lord and
Master this claim cannot cease to be astounding.
On any other lips it would be dismissed as arro-
gance. Small wonder that "when Jesus ended
these words the multitude were astonished at his
teaching: for he taught them as one having
authority and not as the scribes." Someone has
said that "Christ's entrance into a synagogue was

---

[3] So Buttrick (*The Parables of Jesus*, p. 59) translates Matthew
7. 25. The order of the Greek words is emphatic and dramatic.

like the incoming of an eagle with keen eye and
swift wing and bold spirit into a council of blink-
ing and blear-eyed owls." Here is a living voice, not
an echo from the past.   Here is the authority of
one who knows for Himself.   He does not guess
or grope: "Verily I say unto you."   He will even
add to or take from the ancient law: "It hath been
said, but I say."

But never did even Jesus make a bolder claim
than in this story.   He claims that His teaching
offers mankind an indestructible foundation for
life.   In the strict sense of the word His teachings
are fundamental—basic, elemental, the truth of
God.   "Follow Me and your life will weather the
storm.   Deny Me and you must expect disaster.
. . ." It is no threat of punishment.   It is a statement of inevitable consequence.   He was revealing
the mind of the Creator and His plans for His universe, which could not work on any other basis.
For men to substitute their own self-willed plans
was to court disaster.   It must be so in the nature
of things.

An astounding claim!   Yet all history since is
a commentary and a confirmation.   Many who
would not call themselves Christians have admitted
that only in following Christ's way is there hope
for the world.   A John Stuart Mill will tell us
that men cannot form any better rule for life than
living so that Jesus would approve.   A George
Bernard Shaw will declare that he sees "no way
out of the world's misery but the way which
would have been found by Christ's will if He had
undertaken the work of a modern practical states-

man,"[4] or, we might add, if the statesmen would
apply His principles to their problems.

We are still building on sand. The Great War
saw the collapse of the imposing edifice of nineteen
centuries of "Progress." And so little have we
learned the lesson that the few slender gains we
thought we had wrested from the wreck are now
disappearing. Nations resort to the ancient brigandage unrestrained. Alliance and counter alliance take once more the place of the collective
security toward which we were moving. Fear
kills the Disarmament Conference and we begin
again to build up navies and armies against each
other. The World Economic Conference proves
a futility and tariffs and trade restrictions block the
way to world prosperity. "Can any man look
round and see what Christian countries are now
doing and how they are governed and what is the
general condition of society without seeing that
Christianity is the flag under which the world sails
and not the rudder that steers its course?" So
wrote Oliver Wendell Holmes of his days. Are
his words less true of ours? The teaching of Jesus
is everywhere acknowledged as presenting beautiful ideals, other-worldly, Utopian, but quite
impracticable. They won't work.

Does our present way of life, then, "work"?

We today, more than most generations, need a
faith that can outride the storms. No fair-weather
religion is any use in these days. In 1789 a certain
American called Morris, apparently a kind

---

[4] Preface to *Androcles and the Lion,* p. viii.

of ambassador-at-large in Europe, reported from Paris to George Washington, giving his impressions of Louis XVI: "He is an amiable and upright man and doubtless would have made a fine monarch in peace time.  But unfortunately his ancestors have bequeathed him a revolution."

What is the alternative which the modern world offers us to Christ's way?  Behind all our political and social questions today is the issue as to whether He was right when He declared that men and women were spiritual beings of infinite value to God, their Father in heaven, or whether those are right who tell us that man is only a political unit, important only as he serves the state.  Arnold Toynbee has recently said, "The worship of one's country is the most widespread form of religion in the Western world today."  In Germany the right of men to own any higher allegiance than to the Reich is bluntly denied. "Whoever serves Adolf Hitler serves Germany, and whoever serves Germany serves God," declared Herr Baldur von Schirach, the German youth leader, in July, 1936.  The claim of the totalitarian state to make men mere instruments of its purposes is fundamentally irreconcilable with the Christian faith.  "Blood and race" are an unsafe foundation for the world's life.

That issue has been raised in acute form in many lands besides Germany—Italy, Mexico, Turkey, Japan, Russia, all in varying degree have raised it. Our comparative freedom in this country was won by much martyrdom and strife, and it cannot be taken for granted.

There may be legitimate difference of opinion among Christian men as to forms of government and methods of legislation, but it admits of no question that there is a loyalty higher than that which any earthly state can command; that man is a being of eternal worth who will still matter when the State of which he is on earth a member has become of only historic interest; that industry exists for man and not man for industry; that the African counts for as much as the Briton or American; that service and not self-aggrandizement is the purpose of life for individuals and for nations.

In the realm of personal life also there are many voices today to assure us that no rock is to be had, and that in any case the best kind of house is one that is built on shifting sand. For example, Mr. H. E. Bates, in a recent volume,[5] blames Thomas Hardy "for not seeing that Morality, as a fixed entity, does not really exist; that it is really nothing but a fashion, which changes from one year to another, from one country to another, from one place to another, and more especially from one person to another, as surely as the fashion and taste in hats and furniture."

There is, of course, a sense in which popular moral standards vary from age to age and country to country, but to say that morality itself is merely a fashion is to say more than that. It is to say, "Follow the dictates of your own desires; they are your only guide." This is to build on sand,

---

[5] *The English Novelists*, edited by Derek Verschoyle, p. 237.

and there are not a few illustrations in history of the disaster that follows when such doctrines get control.[6]

All foundations seem shifting in these days. To discuss the matter at length is impossible here, but one may record the conviction that the acceptance of the teachings of Jesus in personal behavior and in the widening circles of political and social action offers in sober truth the only sure foundation for human life. It is still true—other foundation can no man lay. "On this Rock of faith in Me I will build," He said. If ever we are to see rise on earth that longed-for City of God, we must take Him at His word.

At least we may set out upon our study of the parables feeling that we are engaged in no dilettante consideration of a dead literature. But if we take them seriously, we shall find our own lives being challenged. What is written above might well seem to some readers insufferably glib. The Danish theologian, Kierkegaard, wrote: "The minister who preaches the love commandment without also revealing how desperately difficult, if not impossible, it is to love his neighbor as himself, proves thereby that he has never taken the commandment seriously or sought to apply it in his own life." Cheap assertions that Christ is the way out are no help.

It is desperately difficult, even when one is ready and willing, to see what is involved in following Christ's way in the modern world. And

---

[6] See further my *Morality on Trial*.

when we have seen it, it is desperately difficult
to follow. "I delight in the law of God after the
inward man: but I see a different law in my
members, warring against the law of my mind, and
bringing me into captivity under the law of sin
which is in my members. O wretched man that
I am! Who shall deliver me out of the body
of this death?" As we look at the state of the
world and then at the ineffectiveness of the Christian community, we may well echo the words of
the apostle.

To an obviously sick man, Jesus said, "Son, thy
sins are forgiven thee." Perhaps we have not succeeded in finding a cure for the sickness of our
civilization because we have not dug deep enough.

As we go further with the study of our Lord's
teaching we shall see more clearly the nature of
the foundation He would have us lay. Here at
the outset we have His startling claim—My Way
or Disaster.

# III

## THE TWO DEBTORS

One of the Pharisees asked him to dinner, and entering the house of the Pharisee he reclined at table. Now there was a woman in the town who was a sinner, and when she found out that Jesus was at table in the house of the Pharisee she brought an alabaster flask of perfume and stood behind him at his feet in tears; her tears began to wet his feet, so she wiped them with the hair of her head, pressed kisses on them, and anointed them with the perfume. When his host the Pharisee noticed this, he said to himself, "If he was a prophet, he would know what sort of a woman this is who is touching him; for she is a sinner." Then Jesus addressed him. "Simon," he said, "I have something to say to you." "Speak, teacher," he said. "There was a moneylender who had two debtors; one owed him fifty pounds, the other five. As they were unable to pay, he freely forgave them both. Tell me, now, which of them will love him most?" "I suppose," said Simon, "the man who had most forgiven." "Quite right," he said. Then turning to the woman he said to Simon, "You see this woman? When I came into your house,

you never gave me water for my feet,
    while she has wet my feet with her tears and wiped
        them with her hair;
you never gave me a kiss,
    while ever since she came in she has kept pressing
        kisses on my feet;
you never anointed my head with oil,
    while she has anointed my feet with perfume.

Therefore I tell you, many as her sins are, they are forgiven, for her love is great; whereas he to whom little is forgiven has but little love." And he said to her, "Your sins are forgiven." His fellow guests began to say to themselves, "Who is this, to forgive even sins?" But he said to the woman, "Your faith has saved you; go in peace."—Luke 7. 36-50.

A WEALTHY Pharisee had offered the remarkable young Teacher a rather patronizing invitation to a meal. He was curious to see something of the young Man at closer quarters. But he was not a particularly important guest, and hospitality need not be strained. It would not matter if some of the customary courtesies went by default.

The meal would be taken seated on mats or cushions, or possibly couches round a low table. As the guests sat with their legs doubled under them, the feet would be behind, so that a servant coming to the table would be "standing behind at the feet" of the guest. The meal took place with a publicity quite strange to modern Western ways. It was apparently easy for a stranger to find his way into the room or courtyard where it was in progress.

But it was not quite a stranger who came in so surprisingly. Everyone knew her. She was the talk of the village, a woman of notoriously loose life. There is no ground for identifying her with Mary of Bethany or Mary of Magdala, or this incident with the anointing in the house of Simon the leper (Matthew 26. 6-13). The name is a very common one; there are nine Simons mentioned in the New Testament. We have, indeed, nothing but conjecture to add to the information given us

here about this woman.   Perhaps one day she had
listened out of curiosity to the preaching of Jesus,
and His message of God's love for sinners had
come home to her.   Her degraded way of life had
become intolerable.   She had recovered her self-
respect.   Her frozen heart had melted.   Her life
had become new.

Full of gratitude to Jesus for what He had done
for her she went into Simon's house to see Him
again.   Perhaps it was a sudden impulse that made
her kiss His feet.   And then her pent-up emotion
found vent in floods of tears.   In default of any
other towel she let down her hair to dry them.
Kissing them again and again as the Greek word
says, she anointed them with perfume.   Her whole
action spoke of complete self-forgetfulness.

It was a very moving scene, but obviously also
one that was open to misinterpretation.   Simon
thought it was more than strange that a religious
teacher should be a party to such behavior.
Surely one need not be much of a prophet to
see what sort of a woman this was.   And yet if He
did know and permitted her to behave like this,
He must have very low moral standards.   It seemed
an unanswerable dilemma.

But Jesus "heard the Pharisee thinking," as
Augustine put it.   He told him a story of two
debtors,[1] one of whom owed about twenty-five hundred dollars and the other about twenty-five dollars

---

[1] It is noticeable how many of the stories of Jesus are concerned with debts.   In Palestine in His day debt was no doubt
as universal and as devastating in its effect as it is today among
the Indian peasantry.

to the same creditor. Neither was able to pay and he canceled their debts. "Which of them," Jesus asked Simon, "would love their benefactor most?" Simon did not see the point of the story, and replied in a rather bored way that he supposed it would be the one who was forgiven the larger debt. "You are right," replied Jesus. And He proceeded to apply the story to the situation.

The story was not so much a defense of Himself as a defense of the woman. With exquisite chivalry He brings out all that is beautiful in her actions. He draws a very pointed comparison between the former prostitute and the Pharisee, much to the discredit of the latter. For this woman had in effect done the honors of the household to a neglected guest. Jesus had been silent when only He had been concerned, but now that the woman is being sneered at He has something to say. There is a whole series of contrasts. "When I came into your house [there is a slight emphasis on 'your'] you gave me no water for my feet, but she has washed them with her tears and dried them with her hair. You gave me no formal kiss of greeting, but she has repeatedly kissed my feet. You did not offer me ordinary olive oil for my head, but she has anointed my feet with costly perfume."

This contrast was not superficial; it pointed to something deeper. "For manners are not idle, but the fruit of loyal nature and of noble mind." "This woman whom you brand as sinner has been indeed a sinner, and a great one. But her

sins are forgiven, and her love proves her change
of heart. Because she has been forgiven great
sins, she loves greatly. Her love, shown in her
actions, is the outcome and the consequence of her
forgiveness."

Did the story, one wonders, do anything to melt
Simon's chilly condescension? The woman knew
from what she had been saved. Simon, armored
in self-complacency, was not conscious that he
needed saving from anything. So he had little
love to give. "Alas! Christ has but little thanks
for the saving of little sinners," writes John
Bunyan. "He gets not water for His feet by His
saving of such sinners. There are abundance of
dry-eyed Christians in the world, and abundance
of dry-eyed duties too: duties that were never
wetted with the tears of contrition and repentance,
nor even sweetened with the great sinner's box of
ointment."

So with kindliness and sympathy for the woman
faced by such a hostile atmosphere, and perhaps by
now somewhat ashamed by her outburst, He bids
her go, but with the assurance of forgiveness.
"Thy sins are forgiven. Thy faith hath saved
thee; go in peace!"

Many sins may turn to much love. So there is
truth in the saying, "The greater the sinner the
greater the saint." But it does not follow that
one can only be a great saint by being first a great
sinner. The great sinner who becomes the great
saint might have been a greater saint still if he
had never wasted his powers in sin. It is rather
that in the great sinner is revealed the force of a

great personality gone to waste which if redeemed might do great things for God instead. The river which in flood brings ruin to a countryside, properly harnessed, may fertilize the whole land. And if a man looks back upon a tale of wasted years, he may be moved to more intense service. "But, on the other hand, let no man think lightly of sin. Though it can be forgiven and swept away, and the gross sinner may become the great saint, there will be sears and bitter memories, and habits surging up again after we thought they were dead; and the old ague and fever that we caught in the pestilential land will hang by us when we have migrated into a more wholesome climate. It is never good for a man to have sinned even though through his sin God may have taken occasion to bring him near to Himself."[2]

And if many of us professing Christians are, like Simon, "such icebergs," to use a phrase of Maclaren in the same sermon, it is surely not because we have no ground for deep gratitude to God, but because we have never seen the truth about ourselves or about the love of God that can love such as we are. So we perform the conventional duties of religion, but never know the abandon of self-devotion. We are possessed by what Coleridge called "clothful loves and dainty sympathies."

If we truly saw ourselves, we should know that we are bankrupt in the presence of God; we "have not wherewith to pay." And if we caught a

---

[2] Maclaren, *Expositions of Holy Scripture*, on Luke 7. 41-43.

glimpse of the wholly undeserved love of God in
Christ for men and women like us, a great love
would flow from a greatly realized forgiveness, and
issue in much serving.

# IV

## THE SOWER

That same day Jesus went out of the house and seated himself by the seaside; but, as great crowds gathered to him, he entered a boat and sat down, while all the crowd stood on the beach. He spoke at some length to them in parables, saying: "A sower went out to sow, and as he sowed some seeds fell on the road and the birds came and ate them up. Some other seeds fell on stony soil where they had not much earth, and shot up at once because they had no depth of soil; but when the sun rose they got scorched and withered away because they had no root. Some other seeds fell among thorns, and the thorns sprang up and choked them. Some other seeds fell on good soil and bore a crop, some a hundredfold, some sixty, and some thirtyfold. He who has an ear, let him listen to this."

"Now, listen to the parable of the sower. When anyone hears the word of the Realm and does not understand it, the evil one comes and snatches away what has been sown in his heart; that is the man who is sown 'on the road.' As for him who is sown 'on stony soil,' that is the man who hears the word and accepts it at once with enthusiasm; he has no root in himself, he does not last, but when the word brings trouble or persecution he is at once repelled. As for him who is sown 'among thorns,' that is the man who listens to the word, but the worry of the world and the delight of being rich choke the word; so it proves unfruitful. As for him who is sown 'on good soil,' that is the man who hears the word and understands it; he bears fruit, producing now a hundredfold, now sixty, and now thirtyfold."—*Matthew* 13. 1-9, 18-23.

59

Once more he proceeded to teach by the seaside, and
a huge crowd gathered round him; so he entered a boat
on the sea and sat down, while all the crowd stayed on
shore.  He gave them many lessons in parables, and
said to them in the course of his teaching: "Listen, a
sower went out to sow, and as he sowed it chanced that
some seed fell on the road, and the birds came and ate
it up; some other seed fell on stony soil where it had
not much earth, and it shot up at once because it had
no depth of earth, but when the sun rose it got scorched
and withered away, because it had no root; some other
seed fell among thorns, and the thorns sprang up and
choked it, so it bore no crop; some other seed fell
on good soil and bore a crop that sprang up and grew,
yielding at the rate of thirty, sixty, and a hundredfold."
He added, "Anyone who has ears to hear, let him listen
to this."

And he said to them, "You do not understand this
parable?  Then how are you to understand the other
parables?  The sower sows the word.  As for those
'on the road,' when the seed is sown there—as soon
as they hear it, Satan at once comes and carries off the
word sown within them.  Similarly those who are
sown 'on stony soil' are the people who on hearing the
word accept it[1] with enthusiasm; but they have no
root in themselves, they do not last; the next thing is
that when the word brings trouble or persecution, they
are at once repelled.  Another set are those who are
sown 'among thorns'; they listen to the word, but the
worries of the world and the delight of being rich and
all the other passions come in to choke the word; so
it proves unfruitful.  As for those who were sown 'on
good soil,' these are the people who listen to the word
and take it in and bear fruit at the rate of thirty, sixty,
and a hundredfold."—*Mark* 4. 1-9, 13-20.

As a large crowd was gathering and as people were

---

[1] Omitting εὐθύς with D, the Sinaitic Syriac, some manuscripts
of the Old Latin, etc.  The tendency was to add Mark's εὐθύς
rather than omit it, especially when it occurred as here in the
Matthew-parallel (13. 20).

resorting to him from town after town, he addressed
them in a parable. "A sower went out to sow his
seed. And as he sowed,

some seed fell on the road and was trampled down,
  and the wild birds ate it up;
some other seed dropped on the rock,
  but it withered away when it sprang up because it
  had no moisture;
some other seed fell among thorns,
  and the thorns sprang up along with it and choked
  it;
some other seed fell on sound soil,
  and springing up bore a crop, a hundredfold."

When he said this he called out, "He who has an ear,
let him listen to this.

"This is what the parable means. The seed is the
word of God. Those 'on the road' are people who
hear; but then the devil comes and carries off the word
from their heart, that they may not believe and be
saved. Those 'on the rock' are people who on hearing
the word welcome it with enthusiasm, but they have
no root; they believe for a while and fall away in the
hour of trial. As for the seed that fell among thorns,
that means people who hear but who go and get
choked with worries and money and the pleasures of
life, so that they never ripen. As for the seed in the
good soil, that means those who hear and hold fast
the word in a good and sound heart and so bear
fruit steadfastly."—*Luke* 8. 4-8, 11-15.

SOME scholars find difficulty in the interpretation appended to this parable, alleging that
it is not consistent with itself, that it does not
fit the parable, and that it cannot therefore be
from our Lord. Admitting the difficulties, or
some of them, I find it more natural to believe
that Jesus did give an interpretation on these lines

which the evangelists inadequately record. Taken broadly, the interpretation seems to me to fit the parable and the situation in which our Lord spoke it.

The difficulties raised by the lengthy section between the parable and its interpretation, in which Jesus discusses the reason for His use of parables, are treated at length in the Introduction to this book.[2]

The parable was told to explain one of the "mysteries" of the kingdom of God (Matthew 13. 11; Mark 4. 11; Luke 8. 10). The word "mystery" is used in the New Testament in the sense of a secret withheld from most men but now made known. Moffatt translates mystery by "open secret." Here the mystery to be explained seems to have been the mixed reception accorded to Jesus by the Galilean crowds. If we are captured by a new enthusiasm or a new loyalty, we cannot understand why everybody is not thrilled by it as we are. Why did not Jesus win everyone's allegiance at once?

A similar discussion is often aroused by the fact that the great majority of the people of this country are out of touch with organized religion. Is it the fault of the churches? If Christianity were only faithfully and clearly preached, would men respond? Is it true that "we needs must love the highest when we see it"? People are generally apt to answer "Yes" to that series of questions, but are they right? Doctor Inge, on the

---

[2] Page 16.

other hand, is reported as saying: "It is complained that our churches are empty. They would be emptier still if the gospel were preached in them." Christianity, he maintains, has always been and must be always a minority religion. Is he right in this?

Quite early in His ministry our Lord was faced by the striking differences in the response He got from different people and even in different places. It is recorded of one town that He could not there do any mighty works because of their unbelief (Mark 6. 5-6). The result of one of His sermons was that the congregation tried to kill Him (Luke 4. 28-30). When men saw the Highest, they put Him on a cross.

This parable was born out of our Lord's reflections on this varying response to His message. It is curiously named the parable of the sower, whereas obviously it ought to be called "the parable of the four soils." There was nothing wrong with the seed or with the sower, but the results were astonishingly different according to the part of the field where the seed fell. To give expression to its life the seed needs the soil. The best of seed will be defeated if the soil will not co-operate. If the crop does not come, it is not necessarily the fault of the seed. It is not always the fault of the preacher if his message does not awaken a response.

The stories Jesus told have a way of remaining true. The four soils are as recognizable today as in the audience that first listened to this story on the Galilean shore.

I

Some of the seed fell on the trodden path
beside or across the cornfield, like some right-of-
way through an American farm.  The path was no
doubt useful, but it would not grow corn.  The
farmer might as well have sown his seed on the
floor of the farmhouse kitchen.

There are people like that.  "You might as
well talk to a post," we say, or, "It fell off him like
water off a duck's back."  They may have ears
but they do not hear.  As the Greek word in this
parable literally says, they do not "take it in."
They are impervious.

Perhaps Jesus was thinking of the closed minds
of the Jewish religious teachers, to which His new
teaching could not find an entrance.  Their minds
were "made up."  But men's minds may be closed
for many different reasons.  A missionary once told
me of an experience she had soon after reaching
the Congo, when she had been thrilled by the close
attention given her by a group of African women.
They leaned forward gazing at her intently and
seriously.  When she paused one of the women
asked her eagerly, "What are those glass things on
your nose?"  Their attention had never really got
beyond her spectacles.

Some people's minds are worn smooth by the
constant traffic of idle thoughts.  They are superficial, that is, they live on the surface.  They have
no deep interests.  They cannot bear to sit still
with a book for an hour.  They would be bored
by a serious conversation about anything.  They

hate ever to be alone with themselves, lest they
should be surprised into thinking. They keep the
jazz blaring from the loudspeaker all day. They
must have something "to pass the time." Poor
things, it is not always their own fault that they
get like that, but it is a pathetic and distressing
situation.

Other people have somehow let the spiritual
part of their natures get so hardened by neglect
that they do not know it is there. They are
not receptive to religious ideas. They do not
believe that the seed has got anything to do with
them at all. Religion is just irrelevant. There is
nothing in them, so they think, that responds to it.

"From all hardness of heart and contempt of
Thy word and commandments, Good Lord, deliver
us."

## II

Some of the seed fell on the stony ground—not
a field strewn with small stones, but a thin layer
of soil over the solid rock. Such places are very
characteristic of great sections of Palestine, where
the rock is very near the surface.

The Galileans were said to be very like these
shallow places—an emotional, turbulent people
with quick but rather unstable enthusiasms.
Others besides Galileans are like that. The
apostle Paul found that the Athenians were given
to running after any *new* thing. But such people
live nearer home still. They are the first recruits
for the army of any new fad in politics or religion
or art. It does not take long to convince them

that this new point of view is the greatest discovery of all time, and they are full of scorn of those who are not up to date. The chameleon cannot compete with the rapidity with which they respond to the color of their environment. "Little pot, soon hot," says the proverb.

They are to be found in religious circles as well as elsewhere. They will welcome the new minister with enthusiasm—so long as he is new. They will respond to a mission, and declare themselves ready to serve Christ and His Church. They are not insincere. They mean every word of it. It is all real as far as it goes, but it does not go very far. Their enthusiasms have no roots.

Perhaps this explains why Jesus seemed at times almost to discourage people who wanted to follow Him. "Lord, I will follow thee whithersoever thou goest!" Do you really mean it? replied Jesus. Think what you are saying. It is no picnic to follow Me. "Foxes have holes and birds of the air have nests, but the Son of man hath not where to lay his head" (Luke 9. 57-58).

The trouble is that the ready enthusiasm and the warmth of emotion which make such people responsive to the gospel make them responsive also to difficulty and persecutions. They are susceptible to religion: but they are also susceptible to ridicule. Persecution or serious unpleasantness would certainly frighten them off, but a sneer or a joke is just as effective as the thumbscrew or the stake. They like to stand well with their fellows. They believe in doing in Rome as the Romans do. They will give themselves to church work so long as it is not too much trouble. They will make a Christian profession so long as there is no opposition. But they have no roots.

Pliable in *The Pilgrim's Progress* was just such a one. He was readily persuaded to go with Christian on his pilgrimage, and he was thrilled by his descriptions of the goal of the journey. What could be more delightful than the cherubim and the seraphim, the golden crowns and the golden harps and the ten thousands of saints? But then the road came to the Slough of Despond, and its mire fitted badly with the descriptions of the Celestial City. So he went away and Christian saw him no more. He returned to his neighbors in the City of Destruction, and sat "sneaking among them . . . and began to deride poor Christian behind his back."

## III

Some fell among thorns. The soil was all right, but it was "dirty." Other things were in occupation. You cannot grow two crops at once on the same part of the same field. You have to choose between thorn and corn.

Men are preoccupied by business or pleasure and have no time to spare for religion. They may be wasting great powers on unworthy objects, or they may be just too worried to listen properly. Our Lord says that the thorns may come from cares or riches or pleasures. The cares may be those of poverty. It is hard for a poor man to be a Christian. He is troubled about the future, possibly even the next meal. He is worried about

the welfare of his wife and family. Jesus sympa-
thized and so should we.

But Jesus often insisted that the love of money-
making and the care of great possessions could be
at least as dangerous an enemy of noble living and
high thinking. In fact, Jesus said it was hardest
of all for a rich man to be a Christian—a judgment
with which we find it hard to agree.

In truth, both riches and poverty, both luxury
and want, suck the goodness out of the soil. No
doubt they are different species of thorn, but they
both choke the corn.

Many of us would have to confess that we
were trying to grow two crops at once. We are
Christian only in patches. We are giving some
of our strength and abilities to unworthy ends.
Our lives badly need weeding. "Create in me
a clean heart, O God."

## IV

But most of the field is good normal soil, after
all. This is not really a pessimistic story. One of
the difficulties about the interpretation is that it
lays stress on the failures while the parable puts
the emphasis on the success. The crowning harvest makes the losses insignificant. Every farmer
expects to lose seed. He knows that the birds
will get some and that some will not ripen. But
he does not therefore despair of a good harvest.

"With patience" the seed will grow. If the
soil will take the seed in, keep it and care for it,
the crops will come, though even in honest soil
there will be differences in the harvest. No man

becomes a Christian all of a sudden.  We need patience with others and perseverance in dealing with our own slow progress.  So many get discouraged by their failures and give up trying.  No man ever became a Christian in his sleep.  The spiritual life must be cultivated.  Yet there are people who devote more time to the cultivation of their tennis strokes or the reduction of their golf handicap than to the study and practice of their religion.

## V

No one parable can tell the whole story.  Can the soils be changed?  The parable does not say.  But the ground trodden into the footpath is the same in essential qualities as the plowed land; the thorns can be rooted up.  Soils cannot help being as they are: human beings very often can.  The hard heart can be softened, the shallow life deepened, the weeds uprooted.  Christ is Saviour as well as Teacher, Plowman as well as Sower.  The same heart has all four possibilities within it.

If the call of Christ awakens no response in our hearts, whose fault is that?  Is it the fault of religion, the "seed," or the fault of the preacher?  Or is it perhaps our own fault, the fault of the soil?

The parable speaks also to those who try to follow the Master Sower.  How do men's lives get like these four soils?  Can we help to make them more fertile?  "The seed is the Word of God, the field is the world.  To know the world, to measure and use its forces, is not to dishonor the seed but to care for it. High-minded ignorance about soils and a fine contempt for the birds of the air may pass for evidence of a spiritual mind, but the result is poor husbandry."[3]

[3] Manning, *The Making of Modern English Religion*, p. 136.

# V

## THE TARES AND THE DRAWNET

He put another parable before them. "The Realm of heaven," he said, "is like a man who sowed good seed in his field, but while men slept his enemy came and resowed weeds among the wheat and then went away. When the blade sprouted and formed the kernel, then the weeds appeared as well. So the servants of the owner went to him and said, 'Did you not sow good seed in your field, sir? How then does it contain weeds?' He said to them, 'An enemy has done this.' The servants said to him, 'Then would you like us to go and gather them?' 'No,' he said, 'for you might root up the wheat when you were gathering the weeds. Let them both grow side by side till harvest; and at harvest-time I will tell the reapers to gather the weeds first and tie them in bundles to be burned, but to collect the wheat in my granary.'"

Then he left the crowds and went indoors. And his disciples came up to him saying, "Explain to us the parable of the weeds in the field." So he replied, "He who sows the good seed is the Son of man; the field is the world; the good seed means the sons of the Realm; the weeds are the sons of the evil one; the enemy who sowed them is the devil; the harvest is the end of the world, and the reapers are angels. Well then, just as the weeds are gathered and burned in the fire, so will it be at the end of the world; the Son of man will dispatch his angels, and they will gather out of his Realm all who are hindrances and who practice iniquity, and throw them into the furnace of fire; there men will wail and gnash their teeth. Then the just will shine like the sun in the Realm of their Father. He who has an ear, let him listen to this."

71

"Again, the Realm of heaven is like a net which was thrown into the sea and collected fish of every sort. When it was full, they dragged it to the beach and sitting down they gathered the good fish into vessels but flung away the bad. So will it be at the end of the world. The angels will go out and separate the evil from among the just and fling them into the furnace of fire; there men will wail and gnash their teeth."—*Matthew* 13. 24-30, 36-43, 47-50.

THESE parables may fitly be taken together because of the similarity of their central themes. They are alike also in their difficulty. Not a few well-qualified commentators have felt obliged to assert that they, or at least the interpretations appended to them, cannot have come from the lips of Jesus at all. The interpretations do not accord either with the parables themselves or with the spirit of the teaching of Jesus. For example, Manson[1] declares that the parable of the tares and its interpretation are foreign to the rest of the teaching of Jesus. They also presuppose a situation in the Church which has not yet arisen, and the interpretation is rabbinic in character.

Let us look first at the parable of the tares. The opening phrase of the parable is curious, but it is common in the rabbinical parables as well as in other parables of Jesus. The meaning is not that the Kingdom is actually like the man, but "rather the Kingdom of Heaven may be compared with the situation arising when a man sows good seed in his field and an enemy comes by

---

[1] *The Teaching of Jesus,* p. 222.

night and sows tares."[2]   The story itself, leaving
the interpretation on one side for the moment, is
straightforward enough and arises naturally out of
the background of the life of Jesus.

"Darnel," writes Mr. Levison, himself a native
of Galilee, "is a very troublesome weed which
occurs in the wheatfields of Palestine.  Women
have to be hired to pick it out from the seed which
is to be milled, and very careful farmers will even
have it picked out from the wheat which is to be
used for seed.  As a rule the separation of the
darnel from the wheat is done after the threshing.
By spreading the grain out on a large tray which is
set before the women, they are able to pick out
the darnel, which is a seed similar in shape and
size to wheat but slate-gray in color."[3]

If this weed does get into the wheatfield, either
from seed dormant in the ground, or from the
sowing of unsifted seed, or, as is imagined in the
parable, by deliberate malice, it cannot easily be
removed.  In the early stages it is impossible to
distinguish it from the wheat.  It is only when the
heads arrive that the difference is revealed.  By
that time the roots of the wheat and the tares are
so intertwined that it would be impossible to pull
up the tares without rooting up wheat at the same
time.

But what is the moral we are intended to
draw?

The parable has been used many times in church
history in controversies regarding church dis-

[2] So Oesterley.  *The Gospel Parables*, p. 60.
[3] *The Parables: Their Background and Local Setting*, p. 30f.

cipline. For example, the Donatists[4] believed
that there should be strict scrutiny and "weeding
out" of the membership in order that the Church
might be kept holy. Augustine replied by quoting this parable and that of the drawnet. The
Donatists retorted that it was clearly stated that the
field is the world, and that therefore the parable
did not apply to the Church at all.

So far as the parable of the tares is concerned,
the Donatists surely were right, though numerous
commentators, ancient and modern, have sided
with Augustine; Bruce, for example, holds that
the parable has no meaning unless the tares are
"counterfeit Christians." The problem posed by
the parable is the everlasting problem of the existence of evil in the world of a good God. How
did it get there? What is to be done about it?
That is an issue with which Jesus may well have
dealt, and there is no need to say that the parable
is dealing with a situation that did not arise till
later in church history.

Evil is not in the world, suggests the parable,
by the will of God. It is due to "an enemy."[5]
But for the sake of the crop as a whole, in the
ultimate interest of the triumph of good, God
allows its presence. He will not destroy evil by
force. Evil and good are so intermingled in the
world and in the individual soul that it is hard at
any period of growth to separate evil and good.

[4] A powerful heretical sect in the Christian Church in North
Africa in the fourth century.
[5] The sowing "while men slept" under cover of darkness is
probably just a part of the story, and does not convey any meaning in the spiritual interpretation.

And, though the parable cannot be taken to suggest this, to render impossible the appearance of evil by the exercise of power would be to destroy that human freedom and responsibility which is the very condition of the growth of good.

It is very doubtful if we have any right to interpret the parable as attributing the origin of evil to the work of a personal enemy of God. Undoubtedly, our Lord does personify elsewhere the power of evil in accordance with the belief of His time. Many people in these days dismiss all that as being owing to the fact that the limitations of our Lord's human life did not free Him from the acceptance of mistaken ideas. Others hold that Jesus was using the popular mode of thought in His teaching, without endorsing it.

However it is viewed, this is a difficult question. The present writer finds it impossible to be dogmatic. The conception of a personal devil is not essential to Christian thought, and raises as many philosophical and religious problems as it professes to solve. On the other hand there are distinguished Christian philosophers in these modern days who find it possible to accept the reality of a personal devil. Further, without questioning the limitations of our Lord's knowledge in matters not relevant to His mission, it is not easy to maintain that this issue is not directly relevant to His religious message. And if He knew that the popular view was false, would He not in this, as in other matters, have corrected it?

So far as this parable is concerned all that we can say is that evil is represented as being ultimately contrary to the will of God, though tolerated by Him for wise and good reasons.

The parable can surely also be commended to the attention of some enthusiastic souls whose zeal is not always "according to knowledge" (Romans 10. 2). There are some folk to whom the denunciation of those with whom they disagree, the hunting of those they think heretics, and the suppression of this, that, or the other vice, are the very breath of their nostrils. They have a passion for being "anti." Is it straining the parable too far to suggest that it has something to say to such people?

Of course we must be quite sure that what we attack is really evil. But even when that is settled, we need to be sure that our method of attack will not do almost as much harm as good. Might it not be better sometimes to seek for the causes of these vices and to go for the causes and not only for the symptoms? Let us beware lest in rooting up the weeds we may not destroy good corn at the same time.

This is not, of course, to justify any attitude of inaction or indifferentism. Our Lord's whole life was a warfare against the evil in the world. By words and deeds He tried to win men to repentance. He did not hesitate on occasion to speak words of vigorous denunciation of wrongdoing. On at least one occasion He used physical force to express His anger, when He overthrew the tables of the money-changers and drove the cattle out of the Temple courts.

This parable itself makes it clear that the divine toleration is only temporary. That is of the very

essence of the parable, whatever judgment we may
pass on the details of the interpretation. The time
for separation will come. The patience of the
farmer does not mean indifference. He will separate good from bad whenever the true nature of
each is revealed and the fit opportunity has arisen.
The separation will not be arbitrary. It will be
based on essential differences.

One cannot help feeling that the interpretation
in verses 36-43 is more likely to have come from
the Gospel editor or from one of his sources than
from Jesus Himself. It does not seem to fit
either Him or the parable whether in style or in
thought. The identifications follow the stereo-
typed formulae of the rabbinical parables. But
however that may be, and all such verdicts are
bound to be precarious, the parable itself is just
as stern and just as decided. Good and evil are
as distinct as wheat and tares. There is a judgment
to come. Not only here but again and again is
that stern warning heard from the lips of Jesus.

## THE DRAWNET

The story of the drawnet is, like that of the
tares, based upon a familiar scene in the life of
Galilee. Drawnets vary in size and detail but
the general idea is always the same. (The writer
remembers watching one being used only a few
years ago near Berwick-on-Tweed.) The net is
cast at a little distance from the shore. There are
floats at the top and weights at the bottom. The
net forms for the fish an impenetrable wall which
closes in at each end as it moves toward the shore.

A large part of the population of Galilee was engaged in fishing in our Lord's day. Fish was one of the chief foods of the people. Tarichaea, at the southwest end of the Lake, was famous for its salt fish, which was both sold in Jerusalem and exported abroad.

A drawnet produces a very mixed catch; not only varieties of fish, but seaweed and stones and driftwood. So it is, says the parable, with the affairs of the kingdom of God.

The interpretation is an almost verbatim repetition of that for the parable of the tares, and raises even more problems here. "The angel shall come forth" applies more naturally to reapers going into the harvest field than to fishermen sitting on the beach. It is appropriate to cast tares into a furnace of fire, but when it comes to fish it is the good and not the bad that should be taken to the fire. And the rubbish from the net would hardly be burned, but, rather, thrown back into the sea.

The parable itself we can well imagine on the lips of Jesus, but the interpretation surely does not belong. It seems much more appropriate to apply this parable to the Church, the Christian community, than that of the tares. The lake, it seems, might be the world. Jesus sent His disciples to be fishers of men. All kinds of men and women would be and always have been caught in the meshes of their activities. Men have joined the church from evil motives. Others have been swept into its range by force of circumstances but have never really belonged. It is just what you might expect, said Jesus. But the time for separation will come.

It is surely not necessary to say that because this state of affairs must have been characteristic of the early Church, as well as of the Church in all ages, the parable could not have been spoken by our Lord Himself. He was drawing a company of disciples round Him from the very beginning, though at first there was no organization. He could not help but notice how varied in ability and sincerity were those who followed. Even among the Twelve there was a Judas. The parable, though not the interpretation, might well have come from Him.

# VI

## THE SEED GROWING SECRETLY

And he said, "It is with the Realm of God as when a man has sown seed on earth; he sleeps at night and rises by day, and the seed sprouts and shoots up—he knows not how. (For the earth bears crops by itself, the blade first, the ear of corn next, and then the grain full in the ear.) But whenever the crop is ready, he has the sickle put in at once, as harvest has come."—*Mark* 4. 26-29.

DOCTOR DENNEY once wrote with characteristic incisiveness of those who betray "an irreligious solicitude for God." They are fearful of the future of the Church. They are troubled about the slow progress or even the declension of the cause of Christ: they are sure Christianity is on the downgrade. They tremble for the ark of God. They fret themselves because of evildoers. And the Almighty does not seem to care.

One wonders if this parable were spoken by Jesus in reply to some such complaint on the part of His disciples. They wanted to see results. Preaching was a slow business. It achieved nothing. Action was needed.

This parable counsels patience and reveals confidence.

(a) *It Counsels Patience.*—When the farmer has sown the seed, he has to wait. He cannot do the

growing for the seed. It is no use for him to fuss,
or to "pull up the plant to see how it is growing."
There are limits to his power to influence the
course of events.

It is the nature of a seed to grow. It springs
up *automatikē*—of its own accord. Quietly, con-
tinuously, unnoticeably, it proceeds with its task.
In due time and order each step of growth is taken.
*How* it grows neither the farmer, nor yet the wisest
scientist, can explain. But grow it does.

Here is a warning against fuss and worry. Let
the worker for God do his share and then leave
the result with God. It is God that gives the
increase. We do not "bring in the Kingdom."
It is in the last resort a gift of God. True, He has
given us our part to play in the sowing and in the
reaping, but there are great processes altogether
beyond our control.

We are always tempted to try to hurry events.
But there are no short cuts in the spiritual world.
Is not that the inner meaning of the temptation
of Jesus? How tempting to try to bribe the allegiance of men by "loaves and fishes"! How much
more practical to fight than to talk, to put Himself at the head of His people and establish a
Jewish kingdom in Jerusalem! How much easier
to dazzle men's senses than to convince their minds
and hearts! To win men instead of dragooning
them was the long way round, but it was the only
way to His goal. There is no short cut to the kingdom of God.

(*b*) This parable also reveals *the confidence of
Jesus* in the triumph of His cause. "God's Word is

God's care." Sow the seed and the harvest will come in due time.

The Second Isaiah had the same sublime confidence. Saith the Lord: "As the rain cometh down, and the snow from heaven, and returneth not thither, but watereth the earth, and maketh it bring forth and bud, and giveth seed to the sower and bread to the eater; so shall my word be that goeth forth out of my mouth: it shall not return unto me void, but it shall accomplish that which I please, and it shall prosper in the thing whereto I sent it" (Isaiah 55. 10-11).

It is only the superficial who can talk glibly of Progress, as some did in the early days of the century. There is no inevitable upward march of events. The world is not going to heaven by its own momentum.

Yet there is much in human history to enhearten the Christian as he watches. We see not yet the full corn in the ear, but the blade surely we can see. There is much of life that has been permeated by the spirit of Christ though there are great areas yet untouched or touched only slightly. In order to escape a superficial optimism it is not necessary to pronounce an equally superficial judgment of total depravity upon human affairs. "Though in the immediate present we often seem to be making no way against evil, a wider and more comprehensive view enables us to recognize that there are silent and irresistible forces which are working out the triumph of good as surely as the seed, through all the changes of the year, is steadily ripening to the harvest."

That is a quotation from one of Edward Caird's profound *Lay Sermons*. I cannot refrain from quoting at some length from his comment upon this parable, especially as this book is all too little known in these days.

(*c*) Jesus bids us consider *the laws of growth*. "The spiritual world, like the natural, has its laws of growth, and slowly but surely within the man or the nation, the seed ripens to the fruit. Inevitably the good or evil act lays the train for the good or evil tendency, and the good or evil tendency spreads out its influence till it permeates the whole life, molding all the habits, all the manifold ways of thinking or acting till the development and organization of character in the individual or the nation surprises us with the full-grown harvest of justice or injustice, salvation or moral ruin."[1]

Often we cannot trace that any growth is going on. We seem to be dealing with small details, seldom with great issues. "Life seems to be a mixture of routine and accident. And we are apt to despise the day of small things, to attach no weight to the trivial round of actions which makes up nine tenths, or rather, ninety-nine hundredths of our lives. . . . But we are apt to forget that life masks its great issues under the appearance of a series of unimportant circumstances and events, in each of which, however, there is some opportunity for the exercise of courage or cowardice, truthfulness or untruthfulness, magnanimity or meanness, justice or injustice, charity or uncharitableness,

[1] Caird, *Lay Sermons,* p. 164.

love or hate. Steadily, silently the 'inevitable' process of change goes on, and neither the individual himself nor any of those nearest to him may notice how, in the one case, his character is being strengthened and elevated, and in the other case is being weakened and lowered. And then if a great issue does come, and he is put to a decisive trial, he is not, nor are his friends, able to comprehend how it is that in the one case he rises to the occasion and shows a strength and resource for which beforehand no one would have given him credit; or, in the other case, betrays a weakness and poverty of character which no one, and he least of all, had suspected. The truth is that the battle is often won or lost long before it is fought."[2]

"As a man soweth so shall he also reap." If you sow a seed, you set forces in motion which will go on independently of you. There will be a harvest. It is true of the individual life, and it is true of the life of the world.

In William Watson's sonnet, "To One Expounding Unpopular Truth," he writes:

"The sower soweth seed on vale and hill,
  And long the folded life waits to be born,
Yet hath it never slept, nor once been still,
  And clouds and suns have served it night and morn.
  The winds are of its secret council sworn,
And Time and nurturing silence work its will."

(*d*) Dodd suggests an interesting interpretation which departs from the traditional reading which underlies what is written above. He would lay

---

[2] Caird, *Op. cit.*, pp. 166-167.

the emphasis on the harvest. He reminds us of the saying of Jesus that the harvest was come and was ready for reaping (Matthew 9. 37=Luke 10. 2). So here, "We must conceive Jesus not as sowing the seed, nor yet as watching the growth and predicting a harvest in the future, but as standing in the presence of the ripe crop, and taking active steps to 'put in the sickle.' " Jesus has come as the fulfillment of the work of the prophets and the climax of a long process has arrived.[3] This is a very attractive view of the original meaning of the parable, and may well be the correct one, though on the whole I find more convincing the one I have expounded above.

Dodd might well have quoted in support of his view the words attributed to Jesus in the fourth Gospel: "Lift up your eyes, and look upon the fields, that they are white already unto harvest. . . . I sent you to reap that whereon ye have not labored: others have labored, and ye are entered into their labor" (John 4. 35-38).

[3] *Op. cit.*, p. 179.

# VII

## THE MUSTARD SEED AND THE LEAVEN

THIS pair of parables may be usefully taken together as both treating of the growth of the kingdom of God, and each emphasizing a complementary truth. The parable of the mustard seed emphasizes the extent of the growth, and the parable of the leaven the method of the growth.

### THE MUSTARD SEED

He put another parable before them. "The Realm of heaven," he said, "is like a grain of mustard seed which a man takes and sows in his field. It is less than any seed on earth, but when it grows up it is larger than any plant, it becomes a tree, so large that *the wild birds* come and *roost in its branches.*"—*Matthew* 13. 31-32.

He said also, "To what can we compare the Realm of God? how are we to put it in a parable?
It is like a grain of mustard seed—less than any seed on earth when it is sown on earth; but once sown it springs up to be larger than any plant, throwing out such big branches that *the wild birds can roost under its shadow.*"—*Mark* 4. 30-32.

So he said,
"What is the Reign of God like? to what shall I compare it?
It is like a grain of mustard seed which a man took and put into his orchard, where it grew up and became a tree, and *the wild birds roosted in its branches.*"—*Luke* 13. 18-19.

**86**

"The growth of the kingdom of Heaven is like that of a mustard seed." There has been a great deal of not very profitable or interesting discussion as to which particular plant Jesus meant. Some commentators need to be reminded that our Lord was addressing a popular audience, and not teaching a botany class. The requirements seem to be all met by the garden black mustard (*sinapis nigra*). The seed may not strictly be the "least of all seeds," though it was probably the smallest of those commonly handled by the gardeners. The references in the Gospels suggest that the smallness of the mustard seed had become proverbial (compare Matthew 17. 20; Luke 17. 6), and it is said also to occur in this sense in the Talmud and the Koran.[1]

The use of the word "tree" may surprise us, but the Arabs today apparently use the word of even smaller bushes.[2] (See article "Mustard" in *Hastings' Dictionary of the Bible*). The *sinapis nigra* becomes larger than the other garden herbs with which it is being compared, sometimes reaching a height of eight to ten feet. Thomson in *The Land and the Book* says he has seen it "on the rich plain of Akkar as tall as the horse and his rider" (p. 414). The branches reach almost the consistency of wood, and birds perch on them to eat the seeds, of which they are particularly fond.

There is, however, another interesting possi-

---

[1] See Oesterley, *op. cit.*, p. 76.
[2] The word "great" in Luke 13. 19 is not well attested in the manuscript and is probably an intrusion. It is omitted by the R. V. and by Moffatt. There are numerous verbal variations in the three versions of the parable.

bility.   Mr. P. N. F. Young points out that in the
passage in Daniel (4. 10-12), to which this parable
makes an obvious reference, it is a dream tree that
is described.   He believes that that is the clue to
the understanding of the parable.   "Our Lord did
not mean to liken the growth of the Kingdom to
ordinary processes of nature—the growth was to
be like that of the dream tree and create the same
kind of wonder and astonishment.   It was as
though Jesus said to His hearers: 'As you would
be astonished if you saw a mustard seed grow into
a large tree, so will you be amazed at the growth
of the Kingdom.' "[3]

The identification of the actual plant does not
affect the lesson of the parable.   Surprising growth
from a speck of seed—that is clearly the point of
the illustration.   What did Jesus mean by it as
applied to the kingdom of God?

(a) *It is an answer to those who "despised the
day of small things"* (Zechariah 4. 10).   Our Lord
had an eye for the meaning and value of little
things—the cup of cold water, the one talent, the
widow's mite, the grain of mustard seed.   A true
judgment will always ask not only how big is this?
—but whereunto will it grow?   What is its significance?   What potentialities are stored within it?
Possibly our Lord is encouraging His disciples not
to lose heart.   "Fear not, *little flock;* for it is your
Father's good purpose to give you the kingdom"
—Luke 12. 32 (compare 1 Corinthians 1).

(b) *It is a revelation of the faith of our Lord in*

---

[3] *The College Saint Luke,* p. 296.

*the movement He was starting.* It was small, but it was alive, and it would grow. In time the mustard seed would produce its tree and shelter men of every nation.

There can be little doubt that the birds of the heaven in the parable symbolize the Gentile nations, as in the complicated allegory in Daniel 4. 10-26 and in Ezekiel 31. 6. That this was the usual symbolism is confirmed by other Jewish literature outside the Bible.[4] "The birds of the heaven lodged in the branches thereof." That is only another way of saying, "They shall come from the East and the West and the North and the South and sit down in the Kingdom of God."

This is no passing thought; it is of the very warp and woof of the teaching of Jesus. He longed to see His people take up in earnest the missionary vocation laid before them by the great prophets and notably by the Second Isaiah.[5]

"Jesus' largest hope was not a missionary few, but a nation of God's people with its Temple 'a house of prayer for all nations,' and Jerusalem 'the city of the great King'—the capital of the Kingdom of God. His Twelve would be seated on twelve thrones judging the twelve tribes of Israel. Had the nation been won, no missionary program would have been needed: every city of the known world was already an outpost of Israel. The Jews of the dispersion would have followed the lead of Pales-

---

[4] See Manson, *The Teaching of Jesus*, p. 133.
[5] I have studied the world outlook of Jesus and of the Old-Testament prophets in some detail in *The Kingdom Without Frontiers*.

tine, and in less than a generation the world would have been evangelized."[6]

The Jewish nation refused His call, and yet language is all too weak to hint at the astonishing fulfillment of that daring prophecy. Probably the only institution that has survived these nineteen hundred years is the Christian Church. It has not only survived it; it has never been, in spite of all failure, so strong, so large or so vital as it is today.

"His is easily the dominant figure in history," wrote Mr. H. G. Wells in the *American Magazine* (July, 1922). ". . . A historian without any theological bias whatever should find that he simply cannot portray the progress of humanity honestly without giving a foremost place to a penniless Teacher from Nazareth." He "finds the picture centering irresistibly round the life and character" of Jesus.

Think only of this contrast. After the end of the career of this "penniless Teacher" all there was to show for His labors, to all outward appearance, was a small company of one hundred and twenty men and women, possessing little between them in the way of wealth or learning or social standing with which to further any campaign. Nineteen hundred years after there gathered in that same city of Jerusalem, at the anniversary of His crucifixion at the hands of Roman governor and Jewish priest, a company of men and women chosen from the leadership of the Christian Church

[6] Cadoux, *op. cit.*, p. 178.

throughout the world. They belonged to no less than fifty nations. To them that "penniless Teacher" was Lord and Saviour, no dead memory, but a living Lord. The cross on which He suffered was to them the symbol and sign of life. Their purpose as the International Missionary Council was to plan for the extension of the kingdom of Christ throughout every land and into all realms of human life.[7]

There is nothing else faintly resembling that in the annals of the world.

It has happened because there has been vitality in the seed that Jesus sowed. "The history of the first group in the upper chamber at Jerusalem has been repeated over and over again; a few devoted men inspired by the Holy Spirit have been the seed of great and surprising developments. Think of the little band of monks who landed with Augustine on the shores of Thanet; of Saint Columba and his handful of followers who rested their weary oars at Iona; of Saint Francis and his first few 'poor brothers'; of Charles and John Wesley with their fellow students following their 'method' of life at Oxford; and remember what great developments grew from such small beginnings."[8] Illustrations might be multiplied from the modern missionary movement, from the story of Uganda, from the immense influence on the whole life of India exerted by William Carey and the Serampore trio, from the fruit of Robert Morrison's seed-

---

[7] For further particulars see *Roads to the City of God*, by Basil Mathews.

[8] Lang, *The Parables of Jesus*, p. 51.

sowing at Canton, from the astounding development of the "Lone Star" mission at Ongole in South India, and from many another corner of the world.

Even when all allowance is made for setbacks in some lands, for the alarming spread of the new paganism in the West, it remains true that, taking the world as a whole, these are days of growth for the Church of Christ. It might be otherwise. These might be days of shrinkage and decline. Even then the growth of the mustard seed would remain astounding, and even then the faith of the Christian in the ultimate triumph of the cause of his Master would remain. There is nothing to be gained by refusing to face unpleasant facts, but neither is there any merit in ignoring encouraging ones. Dr. John R. Mott, who speaks with unrivaled authority about the condition of the Christian Church throughout the world, has several times recently declared emphatically that surveying the situation as a whole these are days of "a rising spiritual tide." Or, to use the metaphor of the parable, the tree still grows and gives life and shelter to men and nations.

In this I have been speaking only of the growth of the Church. The parable actually refers to the kingdom of God, of which the Church is only the nucleus and instrument. If one pressed the argument to consider the growth of the influence of Christ among mankind generally, the verdict would be still more emphatic. God does not work only through the Church.

## THE LEAVEN

He told them another parable. "The Realm of heaven," he said, "is like dough which a woman took and buried in three pecks of flour, till all of it was leavened."—*Matthew* 13. 33.

He added, "To what shall I compare the Reign of God? It is like dough which a woman took and buried in three pecks of flour, till all of it was leavened."—*Luke* 13. 20-21.

If the parable of the mustard seed emphasizes the scope and extent of the Kingdom, the companion parable of the leaven is primarily concerned with the method of growth.

The introduction into the dough of a new baking of a piece of fermented dough kept over from the last one, makes it light, porous, and spongy. Its influence extends throughout the whole mass. So, says our Lord, shall be the growth of the kingdom of God. Put Christians into the world and their faith must permeate and assimilate all it touches.

It has been objected that leaven is always otherwise used in the Bible as a symbol of evil and that it must therefore represent here not the spread of the kingdom of God, as the wording of the parable would suggest, but the spread of evil. Leaven is used of evil in 1 Corinthians 5. 7; Luke 12. 1; Galatians 5. 9. It was forbidden in offerings in the Mosaic Law (except Leviticus 23. 17), and no leaven was to be allowed in the home at the Passover. (This latter prohibition was, however, probably owing to the fact that they were to commemorate the hasty baking in preparation for the Exodus journey, in which no leaven had been used, as it took time to work.)

This objection is surely rather unimaginative. Why should our Lord not be free to use the illustration in a good sense? There is nothing evil in the inherent nature of leaven, though in the manner of its working it might suggest evil as well as good. There are numerous other cases in the Bible where the same metaphor is employed in opposite connections. Two only need be mentioned. Christ is compared to a lion, but so also is Satan. The serpent tempted Eve, but Jesus can use it as an illustration of the wisdom needed by His disciples. Apart from such a demand for mechanical uniformity, no one would doubt that here "leaven" is used to illustrate the method of the spread of the kingdom of God itself.

It is heartening to be reminded that a good example is as contagious as an evil one. Evil may spread like leaven. We tremble at its stealthy, insidious advance. But good spreads in just that way too.

The same kind of perverted ingenuity has been applied to the three measures of meal. Augustine thought they represented the three sons of Noah from whom the human race sprang. Or they have been taken to mean "the three parts of the known world" or "the threefold nature of man." It is much more likely that this was a common quantity for a baking, as is suggested by the reference in Genesis 18. 6. Levison, himself a native

of Palestine, says that it "would form the ordinary
amount of baking for an average family."[9]

The essential point of the parable is simple
enough, though profound and searching in its
implication. In the gospel of Christ a new, quick-
ening, transforming force has been cast into the
life of the world, sufficiently powerful to change
it all.

In thinking of the parable of the mustard seed
we reminded ourselves that Christianity has found
an entrance into nearly every country of the world.
The Christian Church is probably the most international society of any kind in the world. But it
is very far from having leavened the lump. The
world has yet to see what a Christian nation—one
Christian through and through—would look like.
Some countries that once were nominally Christian
have tried to cast Christianity out. North Africa
did it centuries ago. Russia has done it in our
own day.

In both those cases it was done because the
Christianity was itself so unchristian. Why is
Christianity not more effective in the life of the
world? Why, for example, is the Christian Church
apparently so impotent to create a true spirit of
international good will, even between nominally
Christian nations? Surely because we Christians
have ourselves been so imperfectly leavened by the
Spirit of Christ. Ye are the leaven of the world,
but what if the leaven has lost its power? . . .

They asked themselves this in China a few years

[9] *Op. cit.*, p. 40.

ago. Why are the Christians not more effective in the life of China? They answered it by launching a Five Year Movement of evangelism. But they started at the right place. Their watchword was: "Lord, revive Thy Church, *beginning with me.*"

Many of us try to stop the working of the leaven in our own lives after it has got only a certain distance. We do not want the whole to be leavened. To change the metaphor, we welcome Christ into our lives, but we keep the doors of some rooms locked against Him. But sooner or later He comes and knocks at every one of those doors, and there is no peace in our lives until we have unlocked them.

I remember reading somewhere a story about a rather rough, uncultured man who fell in love with a beautiful blue vase in a shop window. He bought the vase and put it on the mantelpiece in his room. And then it was a kind of judgment on the room. He had to clean it up to be worthy of the vase. The curtains looked dingy beside it. The old chair with the stuffing coming out of the seat would not do. The wallpaper and the paint needed renewing. Gradually the whole room was transformed. That is the story of the leaven in another form.

Is there in the parable any suggestion that the leaven cannot do its work unless it gets into the dough? There were many Jews in the time of Jesus who tried to preserve rigidly the barriers between themselves and others, lest the purity of their religion should be soiled and their witness be lost to the world. The modern Jewish scholar, Klausner, says they were right.[10] Jesus, on the other hand, saw not a danger but the possibility of rendering a great service to mankind. Men needed the message the Jews had to give. If they would leave their seclusion, they might leaven the lump.[11]

One reason why the leaven is not more effectual today is because it is not in the dough. There are still Christians who stand aloof, with narrow conceptions of what their religion demands. Some fear contamination if they mix with "the world." Others believe that Christianity is a personal religion of worship and individual salvation, and distrust any attempt to apply its teaching to politics or industry. Surely our allegiance to Christ demands that the whole be leavened. There are great unchristianized areas of modern life which need more Christians and better Christians to take with them their leavening influence. What a ferment would be created in industry and commerce and politics and international relations if Christianity really got in!

Both parables are needed to express the truth about the kingdom of God. A religious imperialism which was content with seeing every country in the world nominally Christian would not be the imperialism of Christ. Nor would the Christian ideal be satisfied by a small self-contained company of wholly sanctified saints. Both extent and depth, both quantity and quality are needed.

[10] *Jesus of Nazareth*, p. 390.
[11] See Cadoux, *op. cit.*, p. 104.

Christ's vision took in the whole of life throughout the whole of the world.

In *Boadicea* Mr. Laurence Binyon makes the Roman soldier say:

"Rome is not marble towers and palaces;
Rome is a thought born in the mind of man
That has conceived an order to endure
Beyond itself. . . .
                              A thought
That moves forever outward, outward, outward—
Cannot be satisfied, till the whole world's
Lethargy and hostility are transformed
Into that order."

"Till the whole is leavened!"  The kingdom of God on earth, in its completeness, is the common life of all mankind entirely leavened by a Church of fully converted members.  It means a world-wide fellowship of men united in the love of God and of one another.  That and no less is what we mean when we pray, "Thy kingdom come!"

## VIII

## THE HID TREASURE AND THE PEARL

The Realm of heaven is like treasure hidden in a field; the man who finds it hides it and in his delight goes and sells all he possesses and buys that field.

Again, the Realm of heaven is like a trader in search of fine pearls; when he finds a single pearl of high price, he is off to sell all he possesses and buy it.— *Matthew* 13. 44-46.

SO the kingdom of God may be fittingly compared to a personal possession, something that a man finds and keeps for himself. This is bound to seem strange to those who think of the kingdom of God as an ideal society, a Utopia. That the Kingdom has its social aspect is clear, but these parables remind us that the root meaning of the phrase is the realm or sovereignty of God, that over which God rules.[1] And unless He rules over the hearts of individuals He can never rule over society. Men must enter the Kingdom one by one. Each must take the oath of allegiance to the King.

Then—grand paradox of the Gospel—by so giving up their liberty men become for the first time free; by so surrendering they become conquerors. For to serve Him is to reign. To find the Kingdom is to become possessed of a treasure for which one's all might be gladly given.

Peace with God, forgiveness, a sense of purpose

---

[1] See Introduction, pp. 20ff.

and meaning in a life that before was futile, good will toward men—in a word, the knowledge of God; that, says Jesus, is the greatest of all treasures. Wealth can be a good thing to those that use it aright, but "he that loveth silver shall not be satisfied with silver, nor he that loveth abundance with increase." The esteem of one's fellows, knowledge, the love of friends—these are great gifts, but even these do not satisfy the deep center of man's soul.

> "From the best bliss that earth imparts
>     We turn unfilled to Thee again."

But with Him all good things shine with a reflected radiance, and we find in them new worth and beauty.

Perhaps none of us sees the truth of this clearly all the time. We are so easily put off with tinsel and paste. Even stranger, there are many who seem to catch no glimpse of these truths at all. They have no sense of religious need, and their lack of religious faith does not seem to worry them at all. They are preoccupied with other affairs of business or pleasure. The gay unconcern of the pagans at times puzzles and troubles those of us who take religion seriously, or even makes us wonder if our own faith is not unnatural and queer. But to some of them there comes a day of glad surprise.

The peasant was not looking for treasure. If he had been, it would not have been in this field. He had plodded across it a thousand times and was familiar with every stone. Yet only a few

inches beneath the surface was treasure hidden by
some fugitive from a marauding band of robbers
or from the advance of soldiers who threatened to
make a battlefield of his farm (compare Matthew
25. 25).  And the gold laid there to be reclaimed in
safer circumstances lay there still.  The owner had
never come back.

But one day the spade or the coulter went a
little deeper and the astonished peasant stumbled
on treasure unaware.  The dull, old familiar field
became in an instant transformed.  Looking
hastily around to see that no one was watching,
he shoveled the earth back upon his find and hur-
ried off to bargain for the purchase of the field
with every penny he could scrape together.  With
the morality of the proceeding our Lord was not
concerned.  The honesty of it is undoubtedly open
to question, but it is the kind of thing men did
and still do.  Whether they ought to do it was
irrelevant to Jesus at the moment.[2]  What mattered
was the man's instant recognition of worth and
his decisive action to make it his.  He had found
unexpected treasure.

So in the spiritual world men have found a
treasure for which they never sought.  John
Bunyan, well satisfied with himself, heard some
poor women chatting about religious matters by
a sunny doorstep one morning in Bedford and

---

[2] Oesterley, *op. cit.*, p. 81, points out that Jewish law on the
subject was quite different from modern Western law.  He
quotes, for example, from the Talmud: "What finds belong to
the finder and what (finds) must one cause to be proclaimed?
These finds belong to the finder—if a man find scattered fruit,
scattered money  . . .  these belong to the finder."

his eyes were opened. Tokichi Ishii, lying under sentence of death in a Japanese prison, to give himself something to do looked idly at a New Testament left in his cell by a lady missionary. He casually turned the leaves. The story of the crucifixion caught his eye—"Even I, hardened criminal that I was, thought it a shame that His enemies should have treated Him in this way. I went on and my attention was next taken by these words: And Jesus said, 'Father, forgive them, for they know not what they do.' I stopped: I was stabbed to the heart as if pierced by a five-inch nail. What did the verse reveal to me? Shall I call it the love of the heart of Christ? Shall I call it His compassion? I do not know what to call it. I only know that with an unspeakably grateful heart I believed. Through this simple sentence I was led into the whole of Christianity."[3]

I have myself known an English convict who listened politely but listlessly to my pleading that his hope lay in following Christ. It was all merely words to him. Yet some weeks later the same man wrote me to say that it was mere words no longer but glorious reality. He had seen as treasure what before he had trodden underfoot.

We may not be seeking God, but He is always seeking us. Saul set out to bind the Christians and bring them captive to Jerusalem, but One he did not expect met him on the road. It has many a time been like that in the history of the Church. Many of her noblest sons and daughters would be missing if no one found Christ except those

[3] See *A Gentleman in Prison*, p. 76.

who set out to seek for Him.  A chance word
spoken by a friend, a turn of fortune, a death, a
book taken up in an idle moment—and He is
found of those who sought Him not.

But men do not all find God by the same road.
There are twelve gates to His city.  If there are
the careless and the preoccupied, there are also
the keen and serious-minded who are conscious of
a need and find it hard to satisfy.  Like Indian
pilgrims who visit shrine after shrine in search of
peace, they enter many temple doors.  In their
ardor for social justice they follow Lenin in the
ranks of Communism.  With the Nazi or the
Fascist they are ready to throw away their lives
if only the nation may prosper.  Eager for spiritual
truth they follow Annie Besant to the worship of
the strange and mingled gods of Theosophy.  Dis-
illusioned by science they join Bertrand Russell in
the chilly hall of "A Free Man's Worship" and
practice a stoical disdain for the universe that
crumbles beneath them.  Or they join the high
priests of Humanism in a religion without revelation, and even at times in a morality without
morals, hoping to find freedom by casting off
restraint.  Others stay wistfully on the fringes of
the Christian Church, unable to satisfy their critical questionings.

In all these realms of modern life can be found
men of high ideals and ambitions who are honestly
in search of what is true, honorable, just, pure,
lovely, and of good report.  Some of these find
at length the pearl of great price which crowned

the search of the merchantman.  Sometimes the
quest is prolonged because those of us who profess
to have the pearl in our custody offer it mixed up
with dirt and rubbish and extraneous matter, so
that men do not recognize its splendor.

Both peasant and merchant gave their all to
secure possession of their treasure.  Theologians
have sometimes seen a problem here.  Do we, then,
purchase the love of God?  Is salvation a gift of
grace or something we can earn?  Surely this is
prosaic allegorizing.  If we must answer, what can
we say but that the knowledge of God is both
a gift and a purchase?  By grace we have been
saved—through a faith that lays hold upon that
gift of grace.  Yet even that very faith is a gift
of God.  Nothing is in reality earned by us;
there is naught in which we can glory.  All, both
gift and purchase money, is the gift of God.  So
one might paraphrase the argument of the apostle
in the Letter to the Ephesians (2. 4-9).

That same Paul who has been quoted on an
earlier page as an instance of the peasant dis-
covering the treasure, might even more fittingly
be compared to the pearl merchant.  He sought
with eagerness to find satisfaction for his soul's
cravings, but the more he sought in the archives
of Judaism the more dissatisfied he became.  But
he found what he sought in Jesus.  And then he
counted "all things to be loss for the excellency
of the knowledge of Christ Jesus my Lord, for
whom I suffered the loss of all things, and do
count them but dung, that I may gain Christ"
(Philippians 3. 8).

So it was with Augustine, another restless seeker: "What I feared to be parted from was now a joy to surrender. For thou didst cast them from me, who art the true and high delight. Thou didst cast them forth and in their place didst enter in thyself; sweeter than all pleasure" (*Confessions,* ix. 1).

The merchantman sold his whole stock to purchase the one pearl, because it was worth it all. In all walks of life men will readily give away the second best to get the best.

Some of us think the price Christ asks too high. With Francis Thompson we fear lest having Him we may have naught besides. Sometimes He asks quite literally for the giving up of family and fortune—as for many in India today, where ostracism and persecution are often still the cost of baptism. But it is no easy matter to be a real Christian anywhere. Always and everywhere He asks for that surrender of the will and of worldly ambition it is so hard to make. It is true that He gives back all that is indeed worth having, but first He demands it all. The supreme place is the only place He will take. And we shrink from His uncompromising demands.

But there are many voices to assure us that if we only knew, we should not think the price too great. There are many who sing sincerely and gladly:

> "Were the whole realm of nature mine,
>     That were an offering far too small;
>   Love so amazing, so divine,
>     Demands my soul, my life, my all."

# IX

## THE UNFORGIVING DEBTOR

Then Peter came up and said to him, "Lord, how often is my brother to sin against me and be forgiven? Up to seven times?" Jesus said to him, "Seven times? I say, seventy times seven! That is why the Realm of heaven may be compared to a king who resolved to settle accounts with his servants. When he began the settlement, a debtor was brought in who owed him three million pounds; as he was unable to pay, his master ordered him to be sold, along with his wife and children and all he had, in payment of the sum. So the servant fell down and prayed him, 'Have patience with me, and I will pay you it all.' And out of pity for that servant his master released him and discharged his debt. But as that servant went away, he met one of his fellow servants who owed him twenty pounds, and seizing him by the throat he said, 'Pay your debt!' So his fellow servant fell down and implored him, saying, 'Have patience with me, and I will pay you.' But he refused; he went and had him thrown into prison, till he should pay the debt. Now when his fellow servants saw what had happened they were greatly distressed, and they went and explained to their master all that had happened. Then his master summoned him and said, 'You scoundrel of a servant! I discharged all that debt for you, because you implored me. Ought you not to have had mercy on your fellow-servant, as I had on you?' And in hot anger his master handed him over to the torturers, till he should pay him all the debt. My Father will do the same to you unless you each forgive your brother from the heart."—*Matthew* 18. 21-35.

PETER has been asking a ruling from his Master about the limits of forgiveness. The rabbinic rule declared that three times was the utmost that could be expected,[1] but Peter is ready to make it seven times. That surely is a generous proposal!

But he is still in the realm of legalism and Jesus never turned religion or morality into a code of law. "No, I tell you, not till seven times, but until seventy times seven—if you can keep count as long as that." The whole question must be lifted out of the realm of regulations. Times without number is the only possible rule.

And then Matthew adds a story to illustrate the divine outlook on forgiveness, eminently appropriate whether or no it was first told by our Lord in response to Peter's query.

Imagine that once upon a time there was a king who was owed by a servant of his a quite impossibly large sum of money, some millions of

---

[1] There is a much-quoted saying to this effect in the Talmud, attributed to a rabbi who lived about 180 A. D. But a much nobler attitude is reflected in Ecclesiasticus 28. 2-4.

"Forgive an injury (done thee) by thy neighbor
And then when thou prayest thy sins will be forgiven.
One man cherisheth wrath against another
And doth *he* seek healing from the Lord?
Upon a man like himself he hath no mercy
And for his own sins doth he make supplication?"

This was written two hundred years before Christ. *The Testament of the Twelve Patriarchs* (about 100 B. C.) contains these words: "Love ye one another from the heart; and if a man sin against thee, speak peaceably to him, and in thy soul hold not guile. And if he repent and confess, forgive him. . . . But if he be shameless, and persisteth in his wrongdoing, even so forgive him from the heart, and leave to God the avenging" (see Oesterley, *op. cit.*, p. 92).

dollars.[2]  He begged the king for mercy.  Given
time, he declared, he would pay it all.  The king
magnanimously canceled the whole debt.  Leaving
the royal presence after this amazing act of generosity the servant came upon a fellow servant who
owed him about a hundred dollars or so.  In
righteous indignation he laid hold on him: "Pay
your debts," he said.[3]  His fellow servant begged
for mercy in the very words he himself had just
used to the king.  But he refused to let his debtor
off and had him sent to prison.

It is an incredible story, and it is meant to be.
It is just as preposterous, just as heartless, if any
man who has received God's forgiveness refuses to
show a spirit of forgiveness to his fellows.  Our
offenses against one another are trivial compared
with our offenses against God.  For all wrongdoing
is an offense against God.

> "The wrong of man to man on Him
>     Inflicts a deeper wrong."

"Inasmuch as ye did it not to one of the least of
these ye did it not to me" (Matthew 25. 45).  His,
as Studdert Kennedy put it, is "the hardest part"

---

[2] It is impossible to determine accurately the amount of the
two sums involved, but it does not matter for the purpose of the
story.  The talent was worth perhaps about $1,200 and the
"penny" about 8½ cents; $12,000,000 against $17.50.  The point
lies in the extreme contrast.  The larger sum is an impossible
debt for an individual.

[3] The Authorized Version inserts "me."  "Pay me what thou
owest."  But the Greek says, "Pay your debts."  He is insisting
upon a moral law though he does not recognize it in his own
case.  "Why don't you pay your debts, you rascal?"  Surely, here
we have an instance of the humor which frequently appears
in our Lord's words.

in the suffering and sin of His world.   In His
presence we are all bankrupt debtors with no assets
worth naming.

When the heartlessness of the forgiven debtor
was reported the king's anger was roused, and
he gave orders for the merciless wretch to be
cast into prison.   "So shall also my heavenly
Father do unto you, if ye forgive not everyone his
brother from your hearts."

In the teaching of Jesus the inward flow of forgiveness from God is impossible without the
outward flow of forgiveness toward others.
Apart from the forgiveness we receive, Christianity is meaningless; so it is apart from the
forgiveness we bestow.   There is no arbitrary
rule laid down by God: "If you will forgive
your enemy, then I will forgive you."   It is a
question of the very nature of forgiveness.   Forgiveness is not a legal act but a spiritual one.   In
essence it is not the remission of penalty—though
it may sometimes include that; it is restoration
to fellowship.   And fellowship with God is impossible except to the merciful in soul.   "Blessed
are the merciful: for they shall obtain mercy."
God *cannot* forgive the unforgiving.   "Peace is
indivisible," said Monsieur Litvinov in a striking
phrase.   So is forgiveness.

If we examine our own hearts, we know that
nothing so separates a man from God as the
cherishing of a hard, merciless, unforgiving spirit.
If a man has done us wrong, as we believe, there
is nothing harder than to expel from the soul
feelings of anger and bitterness, even if we prevent

ourselves from taking overt action of a revengeful kind. But so long as those feelings reign within us the spiritual life is at a standstill. To conquer them, to be able to pray with sincerity for the other's well-being, or to take some positive friendly action, is to find something thaw in the heart.

Perhaps most of us seldom find any real need to practice forgiveness. But so long as we have only to show love toward those we like, who naturally appeal to our sympathy or our pity, from whom we have received nothing but kindness, we have not met the real test. It is a hard test, but it can lead us into real fellowship with God. That is how He habitually acts. "Love your enemies and pray for those that persecute you; that ye may be sons of your Father in heaven; for he maketh his sun to rise on the evil and the good" (Matthew 5. 44-45). "Be ye kind one to another, tenderhearted, forgiving one another, even as God for Christ's sake has forgiven you" (Ephesians 4. 32).

# X

## THE GOOD SAMARITAN

Now a jurist got up to tempt him. "Teacher," he said, "what am I to do to inherit life eternal?" He said to him, "What is written in the law? What do you read there?" He replied, *"You must love the Lord your God with your whole heart, with your whole soul, with your whole strength, and with your whole mind. Also your neighbor as yourself."* "A right answer!" said Jesus; *"do that and you will live."* Anxious to make an excuse for himself, however, he said to Jesus, "But who is my neighbor?" Jesus rejoined: "A man going down from Jerusalem to Jericho fell among robbers who stripped and belabored him and then went off leaving him half dead. Now it so chanced that a priest was going down the same road, but on seeing him he went past on the opposite side. So did a Levite who came to the spot; he looked at him but passed on the opposite side. However a Samaritan traveler came to where he was and felt pity when he saw him; he went to him, bound his wounds up, pouring oil and wine into them, mounted him on his own steed, took him to an inn, and attended to him. Next morning he took out a couple of shillings and gave them to the innkeeper, saying, 'Attend to him, and if you are put to any extra expense I will refund you on my way back.' Which of these three men, in your opinion, proved a neighbor to the man who fell among the robbers?" He said, "The man who took pity on him." Jesus said to him, "Then go and do the same."—*Luke* 10. 25-37.

IT seems likely that Jesus had Himself just climbed up the road from Jericho to Jerusalem when He told this story. At any rate the next

111

incident in Luke's Gospel finds Him at Bethany, which is on the way to Jerusalem from the top of that grim mountain pass. It would be natural for Him to use this illustration for His lesson if He had just completed the climb and could point along the road to Jericho as He spoke.

The road is unique on the earth's surface. In the course of some twenty miles it plunges over three thousand feet, from Jerusalem on its hills, twenty-three hundred feet above the sea, down to the Jordan valley, thirteen hundred feet *below* sea level. In an hour I myself drove from the icy rains of Jerusalem in February to the warmth of an English June at its best among the palm trees of Jericho at the bottom of that "great ditch," as the Arabs call it. The traveler in the parable was certainly "going down."

The road is probably also unique for desolation, devastation, and dryness. It would be hard to imagine anything more sullen and forbidding. Certainly, I have seen nothing remotely like it elsewhere. It seems something of an adventure, even today, to make the journey in a high-powered motor car on an admirable modern road. If yours is the only car you are still liable to be held up by robbers, especially if you are out after dark. The old donkey track can be seen from the modern road, winding its way between the desolate boulder-strewn hillsides. There are rocks and caves in plenty to hide the bandits and to shield their escape.

So it was no farfetched story that Jesus told, but probably a most ordinary occurrence. Josephus

tells us the road was known as "the bloody way."
In the fifth century Jerome writes of a Roman fort
to protect travelers.  During the Middle Ages it
was one of the duties of the Knights Templar to
protect pilgrims on this road.  The ruins of an
inn about half-way down are still visible—the only
building on the road once it leaves Bethany.

In a few sentences Jesus paints an unforgettable
picture.  It is a story that will hold a child, and
yet probes to the roots of human relations.

### THE CHARACTERS IN THE STORY

A man—any man, not particularly important or
wealthy or attractive, and of no specified nation-
ality.  Just a human being in distress.

Some robbers—brutal, callous, desperate men.

A priest and a Levite, professional exponents of
religion, under obligation to practice it and to
commend it to others.

The Samaritan, a foreigner, and a hated one at
that, an alien, a half-breed, and a heretic.  To
make him the hero of the story was like making
a Jew the hero before an audience of Nazis in
modern Germany.  It was like dropping a bomb
upon the complacency of His hearers.  To us the
word "Samaritan" is a title of nobility, but it was
this parable which ennobled the name.  "Thou art
a Samaritan and hast a devil" was the worst abuse
a Jew could heap upon another (John 8. 48).

Of course Jesus is making no suggestion that
all Samaritans were kind or that all priests or
Levites were callous.  If the chronological order

is accurate, it looks as if Jesus were retaliating by speaking good of those who had recently despitefully used Him. (See the churlishness of the Samaritans recorded in Luke 9. 52-56.) Barnabas, who generously sold his property, was a Levite (Acts 4. 36).

## THEIR ACTIONS

The robbers beat their victim and left him halfdead, robbed of clothes as well as of money, unable to help himself, and likely soon to be wholly dead if no help came.

The priest and Levite were heirs to a long and noble religious tradition. The sacred books they honored were full of precepts of kindliness. The Psalms they sang in the Temple services extolled the compassion and tender mercy of their God. If they had lived up to their religion, they would have acted differently.

Yet who of us can condemn them with any assurance? Christians—even Christian ministers— do not always practice their religion. These men had plenty of excuses. Our own hearts can suggest them. "Probably the man is beyond help. I couldn't really do anything for him. And the robbers cannot be far away. If I linger, there will only be two victims instead of one. I do honestly feel very sorry for him, but I must get home. It is a tiring journey, and it will take me all my time as it is. The touch of a dead man—and he looks dead—would involve me in ceremonial uncleanness and the need for purification. That would certainly be troublesome and might interfere with my priestly duty in the Temple." . . . So he passed by on the other side.

The Levite no doubt thought in the same way, with added reason. For he perhaps saw the priest in front of him. "If he didn't stop, why should I?" . . . So *he* passed by on the other side.

How often have we not done the same! Often we are conscious of people in need and pretend they are not there. Perhaps in our comfortable suburb we hear news from pulpit or newspaper of life in the "distressed areas." "Poor fellows," we think. "How dreadful!" But what do we *do?* How natural to call to our aid "all the easy speeches that comfort cruel men"!

Of course we all know about more suffering than we could ourselves help, but are we showing ourselves neighbors to the extent of our powers? Unless we are it is not for us to criticize priest or Levite.

The forcefulness of the excuses for the priest and the Levite is the measure of the Samaritan's courage and self-forgetfulness. He was risking his life in helping this unknown traveler.

The thoroughness of his help is impressive. He rendered "first aid." The olive oil, brought with him for his own food, served as ointment. The wine was used to stanch the bleeding, and perhaps as a stimulant.[1] But he went further. He took the man to the inn and paid the innkeeper to look after him. Two pence was two days' wages for a laborer. He was apparently a regular customer

---

[1] Ten medical words and phrases used in the New Testament only by "Doctor Luke" have been found in this story.

at the inn. He would pay anything else that was owing at his next visit. He saw the job through.

It was personal service, not just the paying of a subscription. It was not merely kindness by deputy. It is good for us to subscribe to societies that care for the needy and probably care for them better than we could. By giving money to good causes we can give our hands skill that they lack and extend the reach of our arms. But the paying of subscriptions should not be a substitute for the rendering of such personal human service as we can render.

## THE AUDIENCE

The lawyer was quite possibly sincere in his question. No evil motive is necessarily implied by the word "tempted," which might mean just "tested," though many scholars think the question was meant as a trap.

As so often, Jesus challenged His questioner to supply his own answer (see, for example, Mark 10. 2-3). If the lawyer himself gave the reply, as is recorded here, he was surely not far from the Kingdom. The first half of his answer was written in his phylactery, the little box of leather he wore on his head or arm. It came from Deuteronomy 6. 5, and was recited by good Jews twice daily. But it was an act of great insight to couple with it the other quotation from Leviticus 19. 18. In Mark 12. 28-32 (Matthew 22. 35-40), which might be another account of the same incident, it is Jesus who makes the reply. But discussion of the familiar *Shema* (the Jewish name for "Hear, O

Israel") and its obligations might easily have arisen many times.

The lawyer was not altogether satisfied with the answer. He wanted to justify himself—to show Jesus that the problem was not quite so easy as He suggested. "Who is my neighbor?" He wanted his obligation defined, made concrete, limited.

The definition Jesus gives is, in effect, "a man who needs your help." He takes the issue out of the region of legal definitions into the realm of conscience and humanity. The real question, He suggests, is not so much, "Who is my neighbor?" as "Are you prepared to show yourself neighborly in practical action?"[2]

"Who proved neighbor to that stricken man?" "He that showed mercy on him," replied the lawyer, who could not bring himself to make the natural reply and say, "The Samaritan."

"Go thou and do likewise." We are part of the audience too, and it is a searching word. To be a Christian involves obligations of human service. The Christian Church, as a whole, has a magnificent record of charitable aid to the distressed, and there is still need of organized and concerted aid.

---

[2] The Jewish law in Leviticus 19. 18 reads, "Thou shalt love thy neighbor as thyself," but it is clear from the context that "neighbor" means one of "the children of thy people," that is, an Israelite. Jesus extends the application even to one who was worse than an ordinary Gentile. His picture of a good neighbor was a Samaritan. This teaching is new and original. It is not to be found in pre-Christian Jewish writings, and Montefiore cannot produce any real parallel in rabbinical literature. But compare Exodus 22. 21; 23. 4.

But Christian duty goes further than charity—though it is a very cheap and unworthy criticism that sneers at charity, unless it be used, as it may be, as a substitute for justice. The Samaritan went a long way with his work of relief. But our responsibilities as good neighbors in the modern world call us to labor to find an order of society which will not produce poverty and distress at all. Ambulances are good, but it is better to have no victims for them to pick up. In terms of the parable we need a police force to protect the travelers from the brigands. Better still, we need employment for the brigands, probably desperate, disheartened, starving men.

## THE INTERPRETATION

Allegory has run riot with this parable. The man is humanity. The brigands are the devil. The priest and the Levite represent the law and the prophets. The Samaritan is Jesus. The oil and wine are divine grace. The ass is the body of Christ. The inn is the Church, Jerusalem is paradise. The return of the Samaritan is the second coming of Christ. Trench, who solemnly discusses this sort of thing, draws the line at finding exact equivalents for the two pennies—why it is hard to imagine![3]

One vice of such allegorizing is that it may well blunt the edge of the story. Here is a story of human need and kindly and self-sacrificing service. It was told to increase the neighborly spirit in

[3] Compare also p. 24.

the world and to lead men to love one another not in word only but in deed and in truth.

To pass by on the other side—that is to be of the company of Dives, and the rich fool, and the unseeing in the story of the sheep and the goats.

To come where the victim lies, to have compassion and to care for him—that is to be of the company of adventurers in Christ's service.  It will carry us today into the realm of social reconstruction as well as of remedial action.

"Go thou"  .   .   .  —that means you and me.

# XI

## THE FRIEND AT MIDNIGHT AND THE UNJUST JUDGE

And he said to them, "Suppose one of you has a friend, and you go to him at midnight and say to him, 'Friend, let me have three loaves; for a friend of mine traveling has come to my house and I have nothing to set before him.' And suppose he answers from the inside, 'Don't bother me; the door is locked by this time, and my children are in bed with me. I can't get up and give you anything.' I tell you, though he will not get up and give you anything because you are a friend of his, he will at least rise and give you whatever you want, because you persist. So I tell you,

"ask and the gift will be yours,
   seek and you will find,
      knock and the door will open to you;
for everyone who asks receives,
   the seeker finds,
      the door is opened to anyone who knocks.
What father among you, if asked by his son for a
   loaf, will hand him a stone?
   Or, if asked for a fish, will hand him a serpent
      instead of a fish?
   Or, if asked for an egg, will he hand him a scor-
      pion?
Well, if for all your evil you know to give your
   children what is good,
   how much more will your Father give the holy
      Spirit from heaven to those who ask him?"
                    —*Luke* 11. 5-13.

He also told them a parable about the need of always praying and never losing heart. "In a certain town," he said, "there was a judge who had no reverence for God and no respect even for man. And in that town there was a widow who used to go and appeal to him for 'Justice against my opponent!' For a while he would not, but afterwards he said to himself, 'Though I have no reverence for God and no respect even for man, still, as this widow is bothering me, I will see justice done to her—not to have her for ever coming and pestering me.' Listen," said the Lord, "to what this unjust judge says! And will not God see justice done to his elect who cry to him by day and night? Will he be tolerant to their opponents? I tell you, he will quickly see justice done to his elect! And yet, when the Son of man does come, will he find faith on earth?"—*Luke* 18. 1-8.

THESE parables are fitly studied together. They have two points in common. Both present lessons drawn from common life to prove that persistence gets its way in the end, and so even on ordinary common-sense grounds it is worth while to persist in prayer.

But both parables take the argument a stage further. The point of both is in the contrast between God and those of whom the request is being made. Persistence prevails on unwillingness, therefore surely on willingness. Both the cross friend and God are able to supply need and both do it: but there the resemblance ends. The judge at last sees justice done, so does God. But how different the motives![1]

To this point of contrast we must return, but is our Lord not suggesting that though God in

---

[1] Oesterley, p. 224, calls attention to the picture of God as a righteous Judge in Ecclesiasticus 35. 12-19, which may well have been in our Lord's mind.

reality is as different as can be from the cross
friend and the unjust judge, there are at least times
when to human eyes He looks like them? "O
my God, I cry in the daytime but thou hearest
not; and in the night season, and am not silent"
(Psalm 22. 2).  Jesus knew that often appearances
contradict His faith in the love of God.  The
doctrine of the Fatherhood of God is indeed
beautiful; but is it true?  We must ask ourselves
if these stories throw any light upon that problem.

But first let us look at the stories themselves.

One is a simple incident of village life.  Unexpectedly there arrives late at night at the door
of a peasant's cottage a friend on a journey who
has been using the cool of the evening for greater
speed and comfort in his travels.  He is made
welcome, but his coming brings a problem.  He
wants some supper, but there is no bread.  Possibly
the host is a poor man who can only provide for
one meal at a time.  Perhaps it is merely that he
has for the moment used up his stock of flour, and
means to bake in the morning.  In any case,
rather than leave his friend unfed he will go and
borrow from a neighbor.

He knocks; only a sleepy grunt replies.  He
knocks again and a surly voice inquires what he
wants.  "Friend," he calls, "lend me three loaves;
for a friend of mine is come to me from a journey
and I have nothing to set before him."

The neighbor is awake now, and in anything
but a neighborly mood.  "Don't bother me.  The
door is shut and my children are in bed with me.
I cannot possibly get up and attend to you."

The excuses seem lame enough. He has the bread, apparently, but bed is too comfortable. He does not *want* to get up. That is the truth of it; the rest is rationalization, as we say nowadays. Was the door as complicated a mechanism of chains and bolts as all that? And the children must sleep soundly indeed in that one-roomed cottage if all that shouting and hammering has not already roused them.

But the host is a determined fellow. He is going to get what he wants. Not content with having knocked on the door at all at such an unreasonable hour, he is "shameless" enough—that is the word in the Greek—to knock again after getting a blunt refusal. And what friendship could not secure, sheer importunity extorts.

The story of the widow and the judge does not seems so ordinary to us, but probably it was all too familiar to Jesus' hearers. Eastern justice was like that two thousand years ago—and much more recently.

The widow is the very symbol of helplessness and is freqently quoted as such in the Bible. She had no "pull." With no protector and no money to bribe her way, her position would arouse pity in the chivalrous. To the callous and unscrupulous she would be a fitting victim for extortion, or at best someone whose complaints could be ignored with impunity.

The judge "feared not God nor regarded man." This, says Marcus Dods, is "a proverbial descrip-

tion for a thoroughly unprincipled man."[2]  He
was a scoundrel if ever there was one—scarcely a
promising dispenser of justice.

To him came the widow.  "Give me justice
against my enemy," she cried.[3]  But he would not.
"He kept on refusing" is the suggestion in the
Greek verb.  But if he could keep on, so could she.
And her complaints got all the more vigorous.
She became a positive nuisance.  She could not
bully or bribe, but she *could* bother.  Her persistence compelled a sort of half admiration from
the judge.  "Whatever will this woman do next?"
he asked himself.[4]  "If I don't look out, I shall
have her coming and giving me a black eye!"[5]
There is a certain grim sense of humor about this
scoundrel.  So just for the sake of a peaceful life
he rouses himself to see that justice is done.

Unmistakable in both parables is our Lord's
admiration for energy, decisiveness, determination.
Ask, seek, knock, He urges.  If asking produces
no result, go and *do* something.  Create a disturb-
ance if you must.  It is a crescendo of vigor.  The
widow's "continual coming" and the threat of
more wore out the inertia of the judge.

Before examining the lessons common to both
parables, there is one feature of the story of the
unfriendly neighbor which is noteworthy.  Is it

---

[2] *Expositor's Greek Testament.*
[3] "Avenge" is too strong a word.
[4] Many of the characters in the parables soliloquize—the Rich
Fool, the Prodigal Son, the Owner of the Vineyard, the Unjust
Steward.
[5] This is a perfectly possible and perhaps the most natural
translation of the Greek.

fanciful to press the point that here is a man seeking help for a friend?    This is an unselfish quest
for bread for a hungry man.    That made his persistence all the more praiseworthy.    The application to intercession is obvious.    At times someone
in trouble, perplexity, or sorrow comes to our doors
unexpectedly.    "Perchance," wrote Saint Augustine, "there cometh some wearied friend of thine,
who, worn out with all the desires and poverty of
the world, comes to thee as to a Christian and says,
'Give me an account of it, make me a Christian.' "
Too often when the traveler comes we "have
nothing to set before him."    Experience proves
how different is the supply of bread and the ability
to help when one has gone in search of aid.

God is ready to help, declares our Lord in both
of these parables.    Trust Him when He seems to
refuse.    What would you do—you who are fathers?
The best of you is sadly imperfect and sinful, but if
your son asked you for food, you would give it to
him if you had it.    You would never heartlessly
mock a hungry child by offering it useless or even
dangerous substitutes.    Well, God is a better
father than any of you—the heavenly, the perfect
Father.    How much more will He give the Holy
Spirit—the greatest of gifts, the sum of all good
things (compare Matthew 7. 11)—to those who ask!

Or, "hear what the unjust judge saith."    If that
callous brute who cared nothing for the widow
or for the justice of her cause, intervened at last,
shall not God, the righteous Judge, who does care,
avenge His elect, His own particular people?
"We prevail with men by importunity because they

are displeased with it, but with God because He is pleased with it," says old Matthew Henry.

Why, then, does He delay? Our Lord does not answer that question, and often we find it hard to find a reason. And if He delays, what good does it do to go on praying, as Jesus bids us do?

It certainly cannot be because we thus persuade God to give what otherwise He would not give. He is not to be worried into doing what He does not want to do. Prayer, says Trench,[6] is "not an overcoming of God's reluctance; it is, rather, a laying hold of His highest willingness." He is more ready to hear than we are to pray, more willing to give than we are to receive.

> "Fervent love
> And lively hope, with violence assail
> The Kingdom of the heavens, and overcome
> The will of the most High: not in such sort
> As man prevails o'er man; but conquers it
> Because 'tis willing to be conquered, still,
> Though conquered, by its mercy conquering."[7]

Nor is it surely because we shall be heard for our much speaking. A mechanical repetition of requests has no spiritual value. The priests of Baal may cry aloud, and Hindu devotees may call, "Ram! Ram! Ram!" but we have not so learned Christ. Certainly it was no vain repetition with the widow. She *meant* it, every time.

We must look deeper for our answer. Does not experience suggest that the persistence plays a

---

[6] *Parables*, p. 331.
[7] Dante.

part in fitting the suppliant's character to receive
the gift? God delays so that it may be possible
for Him to give what is really needed—not perhaps always just what man asks for. It is easier for
a father to comply with his child's requests than
to refuse. It takes a stronger love to refuse or to
withhold till the child can profit by the gift. God
does not "spoil" His children. Nothing could be
more disastrous for us sometimes than to get what
we beg for. How often, looking back, we can see
the truth of that!

Again, there are some gifts that we can only
use when we want them enough. He cannot give
the best gifts except to those who greatly desire
them. Our continued prayer is evidence of our
continued desire. "Longing desire prayeth always," says Augustine, "though the tongue be
silent. If thou art ever longing, thou art ever
praying. When stayeth prayer?—when desire
groweth cold." Our prayers cannot always get a
quick answer, and the greater the prayer, perhaps
the longer it may take for the answer to come. "It
may be," wrote Spurgeon, "your prayer is like a
ship, which, when it goes on a long voyage, does
not come home laden so soon; but when it does
come home it has a richer freight. Mere 'coasters'
will bring you coals or such like ordinary things;
but they that go afar to Tarshish return with gold
and ivory. Coasting prayers, such as we pray every
day, bring us many necessaries, but there are great
prayers, which, like the old Spanish galleons, cross
the main ocean and are longer out of sight, but
come home deep laden with a golden freight."

Delay, as Bruce suggests,[8] may be "the result of love taking counsel with wisdom." The end aimed at might be frustrated by too great haste.

It has been suggested that a mistranslation from the Aramaic may account for the baffling rendering of Luke 18. 8 in our versions, and that it should read, "I tell you he would avenge them speedily, but then would the Son of man when he cometh find faith on the earth?" In other words, God's delays are necessary to allow for the growth of faith, that attitude of trust in God which is the condition of the soul's true growth. God does sympathize with the suffering of men and will stop the injustice as soon as He can, but to do so immediately would be to prevent the growth of faith—the highest well-being of His children.

Even if we do not adopt this reading, the passage seems to point in a similar direction. The real difficulty, our Lord seems to say, is not whether God will do His share. It is whether man will do his. It is not whether God will act, but whether man will be ready when He does. Will there be "the faith," not faith in general, but faith with reference to such a situation as the parable suggests—trust in the dark, hope in the midst of gloom (compare Habakkuk 3. 17-18)? Importunity in prayer shows a confidence in the friendliness of God in spite of appearances which makes it possible for Him to do "mighty works."

[8] *Parabolic Teaching*, p. 166.

# XII

## THE EMPTY HOUSE

He who is not with me is against me,
and he who does not gather with me scatters.

When an unclean spirit leaves a man, it roams
through dry places in search of refreshment. As it finds
none, then it says, "I will go back to the house I left,"
and when it comes it finds the house clean and in order.
Then it goes off to fetch seven other spirits worse than
itself; they go in and dwell there, and the last state of
that man is worse than the first.—*Luke* 11. 23-26.

When an unclean spirit leaves a man, it roams
through dry places in search of refreshment and finds
none. Then it says, "I will go back to the house I left,"
and when it comes it finds the house vacant, clean, and
all in order. Then it goes off to fetch seven other spirits
worse than itself; they go in and dwell there, and the
last state of that man is worse than the first. This is
how it will be with the present evil generation.—*Matthew* 12. 43-45.

A KNOWLEDGE of the circumstances in
which this parable was first spoken would
help us greatly to interpret it. But we have no
clue. It does not seem to belong logically to its
setting in Matthew's Gospel. Luke seems to suggest that it is a sermon on the text which he sets
immediately before it: "He that is not with me is
against me; and he that gathereth not with me
scattereth." That is to say, it concerns the danger,

129

or, rather, the impossibility, of neutrality in our attitude toward Christ. To make no answer to His appeal for our allegiance is, in effect, to say "No."

It is a grim, creepy story—hard to forget.

A house fell into evil hands. The owner turned out the undesirable tenant and did the place up from floor to ceiling. Then he left it, clean but untenanted. One day the old tenant passed it again. He had found no suitable alternative home. He saw it was empty. He went and peered in at the windows and tried the doors. Then calling to him a group of still more undesirable friends he forced his way in and took possession. And soon the house was in a worse state than ever.

An effective story even like that! But that house, said our Lord, was a human personality. The undesirable tenant was an evil spirit which a man had cast out of his life. The spirit came back from wandering restlessly about the desert and found an empty soul. The man had invited no good angels to tenant his life. So the devil found seven other devils more evil than himself. "And they enter in and dwell there: and the last state of that man becometh worse than the first."

Personally, like most who will read this book, I find it much easier to think of insanity and epilepsy and "dissociation" as being the true explanations of the conditions attributed to "demon possession" in the New Testament. The question is one to be settled by the evidence. But it is hard to escape from the conviction that Jesus Himself believed in the reality of demons. Satan was at least a reality of experience. There was a kingdom

of evil to be fought against as well as a kingdom
of God to be fought for, and it seems that Jesus
believed that the kingdom of evil had a king.  He
may have been consciously using metaphorical
language, but it is on the whole unlikely that He
was "accommodating" His teaching to the point
of view of His audience.  If there are no such
beings as "evil spirits," then this is one more
illustration of the fact that our Lord was really
human and did not know everything.  No doubt
He shared in the main the scientific beliefs of His
generation; that seems a necessary part of any
true incarnation.  He did not come to teach us
science.  If He had known the final truth about
everything, His human life would have been totally
unreal.

He was assuredly not presenting a philosophical
answer to the problem of evil, and we ought to
hesitate to build theological dogmas on such a
parable as this.  "For Him evil was not a conun-
drum for the intellect but a task for the will."[1]
I do not myself find that it solves any of my problems to believe in a personal devil, but there are
distinguished modern thinkers who defend the
belief.  How little we know, after all, about the
universe in which we live and about the human
personalities which we are!  How little we can
be sure that our "knowledge" may not be over-
thrown tomorrow, as has been that of our grandfathers and fathers!  Even our generation has not
said the last word.

---

[1] Whale, *The Christian Answer to the Problem of Evil*, p. 27.

So far as the story is concerned, it matters little whether we think of evil spirits or of evil passions and desires striving for possession of the human soul.

Doctor Chalmers, the old Scottish divine, said that what Christ brings us is "the expulsive power of a new affection." He casts out unworthy loves by kindling in our hearts a love for Himself, and that is the only sure way of being rid of them. Many a man has been made to feel disgust with his way of life. He gets ashamed of his bad habits and he gives them up. So far, so good. By all means clean the house. But to give up the old friends without making new ones, to drop bad habits without forming good ones, is to invite disaster.

If a house is to continue clean, it must have a cleanly tenant. You cannot be neutral about dirt or decay. If you stand by and do nothing, the dirt will come of its own accord. The tiles will blow off the roof. The rain will get in. The timbers will rot. A house that is not lived in will begin to perish.

Good forces as well as bad seek entrance to the human soul. Chapters seven to nine of the book of Proverbs tell of the rival appeals of Wisdom, personified as a beautiful woman, and of "the strange woman" Sensuality. There is a temptress who allures to the path of life, as well as a temptress to "the way of Sheol, going down to the chambers of death" (Proverbs 7. 27).

In somewhat similar vein Robert Louis Stevenson tells of men and women in all kinds of unfriendly surroundings "still obscurely fighting the lost fight of virtue, still clinging, in the brothel or on the scaffold, to some ray of honor, the poor jewel of their souls!" "All their lives long," he says, "the desire of good is at their heels, the implacable hunter."[2] Temptations to virtue haunt the heart as well as temptations of evil.

But the vacant soul is a ready prey to the old evil passions and habits. They know their way in, given half a chance. Sheer boredom will urge the owner of an empty life to let them in. The homely saying is true, "Satan finds some mischief still for idle hands to do."

In some parts of Africa and Asia the old religions are crumbling before the attacks of modern scientific thought and modern ways of life. These religions contain much that is superstitious and sometimes elements that are morally evil. But all too often the old faith goes and no new faith takes its place. Such guidance and restraint and comfort as the old faith offered disappears, and the heart is left empty. Sad experience has proved this parable true in these conditions.

The aim of Christ is not to cast out evil so much as to bring in good. It is always better to say to a man, as well as to a child, "do" rather than "don't"; to show a good example rather than display a warning. Religious folk have sometimes been in danger of preaching negations. When John Morley was editor of the *Pall Mall Gazette,* a young journalist applied for a post. Morley

[2] "Pulvis et umbra" in *Across the Plains.* Fine paper edition, p. 199.

asked him what his special qualifications were.
The applicant said he had a gift for invective.
"Indeed," said Morley, "invective against anything
in particular?"   "No," replied the young man,
"just invective."   Some good folk are only really
roused when there is a chance of invective against
something.   They are more enthusiastic in de-
nouncing and abolishing a vice than in seeking to
foster healthier conditions of living in which the
vice would find it hard to survive.   It seems more
than doubtful whether mere "prohibition" is the
way to tackle any reform.   This parable is certainly
one to be pondered by the social reformers.

To fall in love with the good is the effective way
of learning to hate evil.   To fill the day with
healthy pursuits is the best cure for bad habits.
"No heart is pure that is not passionate; no virtue
is safe that is not enthusiastic," wrote Seeley in
well-known and profound words.   No man finds
safety from the love and service of sin except in the
love and service of God.

"Behold, I stand at the door and knock," says
Christ.   If He comes to garrison our hearts and
minds, the evil spirits may peer in at the windows
and rattle the doors, but they will not find an
entrance.

# XIII

## THE RICH FOOL[1]

A man out of the crowd said to him, "Teacher, tell my brother to give me my share of our inheritance;" but he said to him, "Man, who made me a judge or arbitrator over your affairs?" Then he said to them, "See and keep clear of covetousness in every shape and form, for a man's life is not part of his possessions because he has ample wealth." And he told them a parable. "A rich man's estate bore heavy crops. So he debated, 'What am I to do? I have no room to store my crops.' And he said, 'This is what I will do. I will pull down my granaries and build larger ones, where I can store all my produce and my goods. And I will say to my soul, "Soul, you have ample stores laid up for many a year; take your ease, eat, drink and be merry."' But God said to him, 'Foolish man, this very night your soul is wanted; and who will get all you have prepared?' So fares the man who lays up treasure for himself instead of gaining the riches of God."—*Luke* 12. 13-21.

"WE rode by a fine seat," records John Wesley in his *Journal,* "the owner of which (not much above four-score years old) says he desires only to live thirty years longer; ten to hunt, ten to get money (having at present but twenty thousand pounds a year), and ten years to repent. Oh that God may not say unto him, 'Thou fool, this night shall thy soul be required of thee.'"

---

[1] It is interesting in the light of this parable to read Psalm 49; Ecclesiasticus 11. 17-19; 1 Samuel 25; 1 Timothy 6. 17-19.

It is clear that Palestine had no monopoly of rich fools, nor the first century. Indeed, would not most men still see nothing wrong in the attitude of this rich man? It is acting with prudence and common sense. The fellow had earned it— why should he not retire and have a good time?

There is no hint that his money was ill-gotten. It came from good farming, aided perhaps by good luck with the weather. One would like to know whether his laborers shared in his good fortune, but there is no suggestion in the parable that he was a bad employer. Nor does he propose to spend his money on loose living. It is apparently to be a perfectly respectable retirement from active life. And what is wrong with that?

What *is* wrong? In a word, selfishness—complacent egoism. There never was such a collection of me and I, my and mine, as in verses 17-19. It is not for nothing that he "thought within himself," "dialogued in himself"—as lonely and self-centered folk do. There may be no suggestion of debauchery in his program, but there is certainly going to be a very strict attention to his own pleasure. He was the center and the circumference of his little universe.

> "I am monarch of all I survey,
>     My right there is none to dispute."

But whereas Alexander Selkirk in Cowper's poem saw no charm in his solitude, the rich man was well pleased to look round and see nobody but himself.

He was very thoughtful about himself. But his tragedy was that there was so much he forgot.

He forgot in his complacency—or never knew—that he was missing the real "goods" of life. A man's life (his spiritual, human life, not just his animal existence; there are different words for these in Greek) is not measured by overflowing barns or bank balances. A man's real self and his possessions are not the same thing. The Greek of verse 15 is not easy to translate exactly. It might be paraphrased thus: "Even though a man has plenty, it is not in what he owns that his true life lies." A man is what he *is,* not what he *has.* Was there ever a more searching question than this: "What is a man profited if he gain the whole world and lose himself?"

The rich man also forgot the existence of other people, like his brother Dives, who never noticed Lazarus at his gate. "Whatever shall I do with all my wealth?" Were there no good causes needing assistance, no poverty calling for relief, no sick or aged folk in his village? Again we may ask, Did his laborers, his fellow workers, who helped to create his wealth, get their fair share of it? But such questions apparently never occurred to him. His vocabulary is all first person singular.

Again, he forgot that time was not his to control. He thought he had "many years" laid up in his storehouse as well as "much goods." He forgot that life was transitory and his wealth with it. In the midst of his gloating, Death tapped him on the shoulder: "You've forgotten me, my friend. I have something to say to you. I want you tonight."

This sudden call of Death is not a punishment. It is the natural fact of human mortality—inexorable, inescapable, not to be bought off.  Jesus is not trying to frighten people into goodness by the threat of death.  The divine verdict on the man would have been as true if he had lived for years. He would still have been a fool.  Death comes to reveal the true situation.  It is a reminder of the futility of his complacency.  The point is that when he died, the wealth in which he put all his trust was of no use to him. "Whose shall those things be?"  Not his, anyway!

In short, this man forgot the real facts of life. He forgot God, his neighbors, and eternity.  He forgot how things looked from the eternal, that is the true, fundamental standpoint.  *He* said— many things. *"But God said."*  What a tremendous intervention!  For a man to say that he does not believe in God does not settle the question.  He may have nothing to say to God, but God has something to say to him.

And what a crushing verdict!  "Thou fool!" How silly, and worse than silly, is a life that is wrapped up in the love of wealth, the accumulation of things!

This parable is to be found only in Luke's Gospel.  One of the elements in the teaching of Jesus which he emphasizes throughout is His stress on the dangers and responsibilities of riches.[2] Covetousness is one of the greatest sins in the eyes of our Lord—an idolatrous giving to Mammon

---

[2] For a detailed study of this see my *Christ and Money*.

of what is due to God alone.  There is almost nothing He denounces so much as greediness— the desire of having more, not because there is not enough, but merely for the sake of having it. Cadoux quotes a Moslem tradition of a saying of Jesus: "Whoso craves wealth is like a man who drinks sea water; the more he drinks, the more he increases his thirst, and he ceases not to drink until he perishes."[3]

Jesus is sterner in His judgments upon this highly respectable sin of covetousness than upon others more sternly condemned by most of us. He insists constantly upon the deceitfulness of riches and tells us that so far from its being easier for a rich man to be religious than for a poor one (as most of us really believe) it is really only by a miracle that a rich man can get into the kingdom of God at all.  Only by special divine aid can a man resist the temptations of being wealthy. "The rich man, used to finding in his wealth the key to all doors, stands before the door of the Kingdom of God as helplessly absurd as a camel contemplating the passage of a needle's eye."[4]

But while our Lord is so keenly alive to the dangers of wealth, we must not assume that He therefore approves of the involuntary poverty of the modern world.  That is quite a different matter.  Jesus did not teach a sentimental superiority to money and all that money stands for.  He did not teach that poverty in itself is a blessing.  He knew how poverty may turn life into a mere

---

[3] *Op. cit.*, p. 206.
[4] Cadoux, p. 246.

struggle for existence.    Poverty may harden the
soul as well as riches.    Money is not evil in itself.
It is *the love of it* which the New Testament
declares to be the root of all manner of evil.    In
itself it is merely a necessary medium of exchange.
Life itself, and the decencies and pleasures of living for ourselves and for our families are depend-
ent in the modern world on the possession of an
adequate amount of money.    I find nothing in the
teaching of our Lord that suggests that we should
pretend to be indifferent to such consideration.

Whether or not the words following the parable
were spoken by Jesus at the same time, it is clear
that Luke has deliberately placed them here as
continuing the teaching of our Lord on the same
issue (verses 22ff.).    "That is why I say to you, do
not worry.    ('Take no thought' is a very misleading translation.)    Put first things first.    Of course
you need food and clothes and you must think
about them.    But don't *worry*.    That won't help.
Your Father knows you need food and clothes and
it is His will that you should have them.    It is not
that these things are unimportant.    He has made
provision for the needs of all in the bounty of
nature.    If any go short, that is not because of any
failure on the part of God, but because of sin and
thoughtlessness on the part of man."

Many do go short in the modern world and get
less than they need.    But what is the cure?    "Every
man for himself and God for us all, as the elephant
said when he danced among the chickens"—the
game of grab that gives the biggest share to the
most unscrupulous or the strongest?    That has

been one popular method of distributing wealth.
Or the selfish hoarding of the rich fool?

Seek the kingdom of God, says Jesus. Join in
fellowship in common service, and you can all
have all you need. But the team spirit, not the
spirit of the rich fool, is needed. He said, "my
goods," because he was a fool. Jesus would
have us say, "our daily bread." Then there would
be enough for all. This is not the place to discuss
the political and economic methods by which such
changes may be brought about that the wealth of
society may be fairly shared. I have said a good
deal about this in *Christ and Money,* to which
reference has already been made. But we may
well look again at the warnings and advice of our
Lord—unheeded yet.

Mr. Tawney has dubbed our whole modern
civilization *The Acquisitive Society,* and tells us
that greed is the motive power to which we trust
for its working. That is a stern judgment and needs
qualification such as Mr. Tawney himself gives it.
Much of the best work of the world is not done
for money at all, and even in commerce and industry, where the temptation is strongest, there are
many business men, big and small, for whom the
thought of profit is by no means the governing
consideration.

But in general the charge is uncomfortably true.
As a society we have wrong standards of judgment.
Money counts too highly. We do rely on motives
of gain and loss more than we need or should.
Certainly, behind many tragedies is the desire to
get rich quickly. Behind the financial crashes

which from time to time startle us and which bring ruin to many innocent people is the sin of covetousness. Such crashes are symptomatic of much that is hidden from the general public.

Or, if we consider society on a larger scale, who can doubt that covetousness has been behind many of the military adventures of the past in the undeveloped regions of the earth, as it was behind the lawless act of brigandage on the part of Italy which shocked the conscience of the world? For the world is now happily ready to be shocked by actions which former generations took for granted.

Any attempt on the part of a powerful nation to corner for its own profit the necessary wealth of the world will always have in it the seeds of war. The offer made by the British Government in Geneva that the British nation, which has acquired in past centuries by fair means and foul a lion's share of the world's resources, was willing to discuss proposals for their more equitable sharing with other nations, is at least a step on the right road. The public opinion of the country ought to be ready for any immediate sacrifices which this policy might involve. I write immediate, because in the long run this is the way to peace and prosperity.

Let us seek first the kingdom of God—live in the spirit of Christ. So all these things, food and clothing, peace and plenty, shall be added unto us. But let us beware of covetousness. That means the denial of brotherhood, extremes of wealth and poverty, economic disaster and war.

It is easy to join with some enthusiasm in a chorus of disapproval of the rich fool, because there is no danger that *we* shall ever have too much money. But this is not, in fact, a rich man's problem alone. Covetousness has its roots in all of us. A poor man may be a worshiper of Mammon and a rich man may not. It is part of the deceitfulness of riches that men do not recognize their condition. Francis Xavier once said that men had confessed to him in the confessional every imaginable sin, but that no one had ever confessed that he was covetous.

The fundamental question for any man is whether he is going to take the acquisitive view of life or the creative—the generous; whether he is out to get or to give; whether he is in life for what he can make or for what he can contribute; whether his business, whatever it be, is a public service or merely a means of private gain. We ought to be able to say to our children that we would rather see them poor but serving their fellows than wealthy and exploiting them—and *we ought to mean it*.

To live to get is to miss, with the rich fool, the real goods of life and to prevent others from having them. Money is valuable only as it provides, or makes possible, true wealth—love, friendship, appreciation of the good, the true, the beautiful. The rights of property in any Christian order of society would be subordinated to the rights of human well-being. Covetousness is folly because it grasps at money under the impression that it means life.

Mammon, declares Milton in *Paradise Lost,* was the most despicable of all the fallen angels,

> "The least erected spirit that fell
> From heaven; for e'en in heaven his looks and thoughts
> Were always downward bent, admiring more
> The riches of heaven's pavement, trodden gold,
> Than ought divine or holy else enjoyed
> In vision beatific."

A man is what he *is,* not what he *has.* He may own shelves full of the classics bound in the best morocco and be illiterate; he may cover his walls with square yards of "old masters" and have no love of beauty. He may possess acres of soil or a whole fleet of motor cars and be small-minded.

When death comes and strips from us all we own, what shall we still have left? There is a wealth that no man, and not death itself, can take from us. To put into wider currency among mankind the gold of friendship and fair dealing, to push out of circulation the base coin of selfishness, hatred, and lust, to do justly, to love mercy and to walk humbly with our God—that is to have treasure in heaven and to be rich toward God.

# XIV

## THE BARREN FIG TREE

And he told this parable. "A man had a fig tree planted in his vineyard; he came in search of fruit on it but he found none. So he said to the vinedresser, 'Here have I come for three years in search of fruit on this fig tree without finding any; cut it down, why should it take up space?' But the man replied, 'Leave it for this year, sir, till I dig round about it and put in manure. Then it may bear fruit next year. If not, you can have it cut down.' "—*Luke* 13. 6-9.

THE business of a fig tree is to bear figs. If it ceases to do that, it has lost its reason for existing. So a nation, or a man, has to justify its existence. It too has to "bear fruit." To be useless is to come under the divine judgment. Yet God is infinitely patient and will not give up until all possibility of fruitfulness is gone. We might give this parable a subtitle: The Parable of the Second Chance.

There is nothing extraordinary about the presence of a fig tree in a vineyard. Fig trees and olive trees are commonly enough planted there in the East. They are a stand-by if the vineyard has a bad year, and a welcome supplement to its produce at any time. It is, therefore, beside the point to seek the lesson of the parable, as some have done, in the fact that the fig tree does not really belong to its surroundings, that it has no natural or necessary place in a vineyard but is there only on sufferance. It is no more on sufferance than are the vines, which would be removed just as quickly if they ceased to bear fruit.

It is also straining the parable to see in it an evidence of the universalizing of Christianity; the tree of Judaism is to go to make room for another more fruitful Gentile tree.

It is probably also very precarious to interpret the parable in the light of the incident recorded in the preceding verses. Doubtless there was a connection in the mind of the editor of the Gospel, but we cannot be at all sure that the parable was spoken at the same time.

But surely here there is no need to search for subtleties. The message of the story is searching but not hard to find. Nation, man, and tree alike are justified by what they are and do. The ax of judgment falls upon the useless tree, but not until the gardener has given it every chance.

The primary reference is probably to the Jewish nation, making so disappointing a response to the divine care. Once again in this parable there sounds that recurring note of crisis. By their attitude toward God's appeal in Jesus will the nation be judged. Here is another chance for them. They have stoned the prophets. Will they listen to the Son? If not, the end is near—not through a divine vengeance for their rejection of Jesus, but as the inevitable result of facts, as much in the nature of things as the cutting down of a useless fruit tree.

But the parable applied just as searchingly to
the individual men and women who listened to
Jesus, and it applies to us and to all men.

The tree was not only useless, it cumbered the
ground. It took up a place that could be more
usefully employed. Possibly it was also doing
positive harm to the ground, sucking up its goodness to no profit. There can be no more scathing
verdict on a man than that things would get on
better if he were not there. Sometimes a man who
is obviously wasting his life will respond in irrita-
tion to any protest, that, after all, it is his own business; he is harming nobody but himself. But we
cannot live to ourselves like that. Even if it were
true that the man was harming only himself, it
would still be the business of the Christian to
try to save him from himself. But, in fact, the
wasted life cumbers the ground. A slacker infects
those about him. A dissolute man can lower the
tone of an office or a shop. If we fail to do our
job, we are making it harder for others to do
theirs.

This may be, from one point of view, the
parable of the second chance. But there are
stern possibilities in it too. There may come
a time when the tree must be cut down. The
Jewish nation was cast from its vineyard. It
turned a deaf ear to warnings, and calamity came.
"Too late" must sometimes be spoken of a nation,
and sometimes, so far as the human judgment can
see, of a man. There is nothing more that even
God can do for him. He is useless.

And yet I believe that the emphasis of the parable lies rather on the renewal of opportunity than upon final doom. God will never give up so long as there is hope.

In *God's Search for Man,* a composite volume by Karl Barth and Eduard Thurneysen, there is a searching sermon on "The New Beginning." "Listen! 'Unless you turn and become as little children.' What does that mean? Surely something! It means—we cannot understand this otherwise—it must mean, 'There is, yes, there is a possibility of going back.' There is such a thing as a new beginning! There is possibility, hope, future, youth—yes, and for us, precisely for those of us who have become stuck fast, who have run ourselves into a corner, who have grown old, even standing at death's door. Jesus does not try to fool us. When He says, 'Unless you turn and become as little children,' He means, 'You can, you may—go do it!' That is Jesus, through whom, for whose sake, in whose presence there is this possibility of a new beginning in a life that has already grown old. . . . To come to Jesus means to let Him tell us that. . . .

"There is a new beginning, and a new creation possible in Jesus Christ, which reaches clear down where we are fettered in body and soul—yes, into sickness, and life's very need. We can! Oh, let us hear, let the Gospels tell us, 'We can!' Now, do not interpose immediately and say, 'No, I cannot; I am too old; too fossilized; nothing in life can be made new again.' Indeed it can! This is the grace of God in Christ which frees us from the old hopeless idea which says: 'No use to try; I simply can't.'   Certainly you can!   Rise up and walk.   Christ gives you hope and a future.   Oh that we could only hear and see that!"[1]

There is a second chance.

---

[1] *Op. cit.,* pp. 160-162.

## XV

# THE MARRIAGE OF THE KING'S SON AND THE GREAT SUPPER

Then Jesus again addressed them in parables. "The Realm of heaven," he said, "may be compared to a king who gave a marriage-banquet in honor of his son. He sent his servants to summon the invited guests to the feast, but they would not come. Once more he sent some other servants saying, 'Tell the invited guests, here is my supper all prepared, my oxen and fat cattle are killed, everything is ready; come to the marriage-banquet.' But they paid no attention and went off, one to his estate, another to his business, while the rest seized his servants and ill-treated them and killed them. The king was enraged; he sent his troops and destroyed those murderers and burned up their city. Then he said to his servants, 'The marriage-banquet is all ready, but the invited guests did not deserve it. So go to the byeways and invite anyone you meet to the marriage-banquet.' And those servants went out on the roads and gathered all they met, bad and good alike. Thus the marriage-banquet was supplied with guests. Now when the king came in to view his guests, he saw a man there who was not dressed in a wedding-robe. So he said to him, 'My man, how did you get in here without a wedding-robe?' The man was speechless. Then said the king to his servants, 'Take him hand and foot, and throw him outside, out into the darkness; there men will wail and gnash their teeth. For many are invited but few are chosen."—*Matthew* 22. 1-14.

He also told a parable to the guests, when he observed how they picked out the best places. "When anyone invites you to a marriage-banquet," he said, "never lie down in the best place, in case a more distinguished guest than yourself has been invited; then the host will tell you, 'Make room for him,' and you will proceed in shame to take the lowest place. No, when you are invited, go and recline in the lowest place, so that when your host comes in he will tell you, 'Move higher up, my friend.' Then you will be honored before your fellow guests.

"For everyone who uplifts himself will be humbled, and he who humbles himself will be uplifted."

He also said to his host, "When you give a dinner or supper, do not ask your friends or your brothers or your relatives or your rich neighbors, in case they invite you back again and you get repaid. No, when you give a banquet, invite the poor, the maimed, the lame, and the blind. Then you will be blessed; for as they have no means of repaying you, you will be repaid at the resurrection of the just." Hearing this, one of his fellow guests said to him, "Blessed is he who feasts in the Realm of God!" Jesus said to him, "There was a man who was giving a large supper, to which he had invited a number of guests. At the hour for supper he sent his servant to tell the guests, 'Come, things are all ready.' But they all alike proceeded to decline. The first said to him, 'I have bought a farm and I am obliged to go and look at it. Pray consider me excused.' The second said, 'I have bought five pair of oxen and I am going to try them. Pray consider me excused.' Another said, 'I have married a wife; that is why I cannot come.' The servant went and reported this to his master. Then the master of the house was enraged, and said to his servant, 'Quick, go out to the streets and lanes of the town and bring in the poor, the maimed, the blind, and the lame.' When the servant announced, 'Your order has been carried out, sir, but there is still room,' the master said to the servant, 'Go out to the roads and hedges and make people come in, to fill up my house. For I tell you that not one of those who were invited shall taste my supper.' "— *Luke* 14. 7-24.

NO one can read the story of the Marriage of the King's Son attentively without realizing that some mishap has befallen it. Frankly, it does not make sense as it now stands in Matthew's Gospel. It is idle to conjecture how it happened, but it seems clear that portions of three separate parables have been mixed together.

Let us look at the incongruities. In the first place, the story of the man without a wedding garment, which in itself is difficult enough, as we shall see, becomes still more difficult if it is attached to the present story. We may conjecture that it was perhaps the conclusion of another story the beginning of which has been lost.

Much more perplexing, however, is the account of the military expedition. Verses 6 and 7 seem an unintelligible intrusion into the story of the feast. Who are "the rest" in verse 6, and why should they respond in such an outrageous fashion to an invitation to a wedding? One could understand a refusal of the invitation, but the killing of the servants is incomprehensible. Still more puzzling is the carrying out of a punitive expedition while the dinner is still on the table. The army is sent out, destroys the murderers, burns their city—surely the city in which king and guests resided—and then returns. And then the king proceeds with the interrupted feast!

If verses 6 and 7 and verses 11 to 14 are omitted,

we are left with a consecutive and convincing story.

With the excision of the intruding verses the stories in Matthew and Luke are revealed as essentially the same. Luke's version merely adds vivid detail to the basic narrative. Some such solution to the otherwise inexplicable problem seems to be increasingly commending itself to New Testament scholars.

It has been suggested, for example, by Wellhausen that verses 6 and 7 are an editorial addition after the destruction of Jerusalem. Other scholars, more plausibly, believe that two parables have somehow got mixed together. Manson agrees with Harnack in suggesting that there was another parable akin to that of the vineyard which was conflated with the parable of the great feast which we have in Luke. In rough outline it told of a king who gave a marriage feast for his son. He sends servants to call the guests. But the guests maltreat and kill the messengers. Whereupon the king sends his armies to punish the murderers.[1]

On this assumption that verses 6 and 7 are an intrusion, however that may be accounted for, we may proceed to examine the story of the great feast, essentially the same in Matthew and in Luke, and then separately, the incident of the man without the wedding garment.

Two small points may be dealt with first. The sending of messengers to carry the invitation, especially to the more honored guests, seems

[1] T. W. Manson, *The Teaching of Jesus*, pp. 83-86.

strange to us, but many instances could be quoted. For example, Mr. Levison, himself brought up in Galilee, states that it is quite usual even in modern times.[2]    There are several similar incidents in Shakespeare's plays, for example, *Romeo and Juliet,* Act ii, scene 2, where Capulet gives his servant a list of people to be invited to a feast at his house that night.

> "Go, sirrah, trudge about
> Through fair Verona; find those persons out
> Whose names are written there, and to them say,
> My house and welcome on their pleasure stay."

To turn to the other point, Luke 14. 23 has had an unhappy notoriety as an alleged justification for the use of persecution and compulsion in religion: "Compel them to come in" (R. V., "Constrain"). Surely, this is a perverse application if ever there was one.   How much compulsion would a starving beggar need to induce him to partake of a free dinner?   Just enough to overcome his initial incredulity that the invitation was really meant for him!

That leads naturally to the main theme of the parable—for we are treating the two as one.   It is the reluctance of men to accept the offer of God's bounty.   According to Luke's version our Lord was dining with a Pharisee, and had been urging His host to extend his hospitality to the poor and not only to his friends and rich neighbors.   They might ask you back again, He suggests ironically. Apparently, these remarks created a rather awk-

---

[2] *The Parables: Their Background and Local Setting,* p. 232.

ward atmosphere.  This criticism of social custom
and the selfish habits of the rich seemed out of
place.  So one of the guests came to the rescue with
a pious remark intended to divert the conversation
into safer channels: "Blessed is he that shall eat
bread in the kingdom of God."  The remark
sounded well and the guest hoped it would pass.
But such insincere religiosity could not be over-
looked, and our Lord proceeded to tell another
story to show that in reality when God invites men
to the feast, they do not want it.

It is interesting, by the way, to find here, as not
infrequently in the Bible, response to the divine
call upon our lives compared with a banquet.
Religion is often thought of merely in terms of
duty and sacrifice; it is also, and indeed primarily,
the acceptance of undeserved bounty at God's
hand, an entering into joy.

But the main point in the parable lies in the
excuses offered for the rejection of the royal
invitation.  Of course no one would so treat a
royal command to attend a banquet.  Is it not,
indeed, part of Jesus' aim to suggest how stupidly
men do behave when God invites?

On sober review the excuses appear as flimsy
pretexts.  The real reason was simply that those
invited did not want to come.  They were preoccupied with other matters, all legitimate in
themselves, but allowed to obscure the honor of
the royal invitation, and the rudeness, and worse,
of so refusing it.

The excuses are samples of the pleasures and
affairs that occupy heart and life.  Probably few

men and women in our modern world consider the claims of God with seriousness and then deliberately reject them. They, rather, allow themselves to be so preoccupied with business and sport and social life that religion gets crowded out. They hardly realize that any invitation has been issued to them at all. They do not consciously ask the questions that religion answers. They do not feel the need of the food it offers. Religion is all right, no doubt, for those who have nothing better to do.

The kingdom of God is not for those who are content without it. It is for the hungry, not for the satisfied. If the wealthy and the conventionally religious reject God's invitation—those who sat at meat with Jesus round that Pharisee's table, and others like them—there are plenty of others who will respond to the invitation. God's messengers will go to the needy and the outcast, the publican and the sinner, and lovingly assure these bewildered and incredulous "outsiders" that the palace doors have been thrown open for them.

## THE WEDDING GARMENT

These verses, as has been pointed out, are clearly not sense as they stand. As Streeter remarks: "How could the man just swept in from the highways be expected to have on a wedding garment?"[3] If, however, the verses be detached from their present setting, we can imagine a story of a man duly invited to a royal wedding feast who

---

[3] *The Four Gospels*, p. 243.

came without troubling to dress himself suitably. His presence on such an occasion in his rough working clothes could only be regarded as an insult to his host. He is there only for the food and drink, and not as a true guest to share in the rejoicing. It is clearly implied (verse 12) that the man had no reasonable excuse. The king is naturally angry and causes the man to be flung into the narrow unlit street outside the warmth and brightness of the banqueting hall.

I have failed to find any real evidence for the frequently repeated assertion that it was the custom for the host to supply on the spot a special "wedding garment," and that the man had refused to put it on.

It is idle to seek too curiously for the meaning of what is clearly only a fragment of a parable.

Oesterley quotes interesting illustrations from rabbinic literature in which a similar theme is employed. Rabbi Jochanan (second half of first century A. D.) told a parable about a king who invited his servants to a feast without fixing the exact time for its beginning. The wise ones dressed themselves and waited ready at the entrance of the palace. The foolish ones went on with their ordinary work. Suddenly the invitation came, and the foolish ones had to enter the royal presence, dirty as they were. The king angrily ordered them to stand and watch while those who were decently dressed consumed the feast. A similar story is also quoted from Rabbi Judah La-Nasi, who lived about 200 A. D.[4]

---

[4] *The Gospel Parables*, pp. 128ff.

# XVI

## THE LOST SHEEP AND THE LOST COIN

Now the taxgatherers and sinners were all approaching him to listen to him, but the Pharisees and the scribes complained, "He welcomes sinners and eats along with them!" So he told them this parable: "Which of you with a hundred sheep, if he loses one, does not leave the ninety-nine in the desert and go after the lost one till he finds it? When he finds it he puts it on his shoulders with joy, and when he gets home he gathers his friends and neighbors: 'Rejoice with me,' he says to them, 'for I have found the sheep I lost.' So, I tell you, there will be joy in heaven over a single sinner who repents, more than over ninety-nine good people who do not need to repent."—*Luke* 15. 1-7.

Tell me, if a man has a hundred sheep and one of them strays, will he not leave the ninety-nine sheep on the hills and go in search of the one that has strayed? And if he happens to find it, I tell you he rejoices over it more than over the ninety-nine that never went astray. So it is not the will of your Father in heaven that a single one of these little ones should be lost.— *Matthew* 18. 12-14.

Or again, suppose a woman has ten shillings. If she loses one of them, does she not light a lamp and scour the house and search carefully till she finds it? And when she finds it she gathers her women friends and neighbors, saying, "Rejoice with me, for I have found the shilling I lost." So, I tell you, there is joy in the presence of the angels of God over a single sinner who repents.—*Luke* 15. 8-10.

WHOEVER sits down to write about the fif-
teenth chapter of Saint Luke's Gospel must
find himself the prey of conflicting emotions.

On the one hand he feels that volumes could
not do justice to the wealth that is here displayed.
For sheer artistry these stories are among the greatest in the world's literature.   They are fascinating.
One could willingly dwell on the consummate skill
of the character drawing, where every phrase tells,
and upon the dramatic fitness of every line.  Again,
each of these tales is a window into a world of
ancient Eastern life that invites the closest exam-
ination; and much might be written in explanation.  Yet again, this chapter reveals the mind of
Jesus, the friend of publicans and sinners, so that
whole books might be written on that theme alone
with these words as text.  These stories are revolutionary in their revelation of the nature of the
eternal God; revolutionary because they upset
not only the theologies of ancient Judaism
but many of the theologies that have claimed to
be Christian.  The more they are studied, the
more they blaze with light upon human life and
destiny.

But, on the other hand, the would-be commen-
tator shrinks from his task in despair.  To write
anything at all is "to gild refined gold, to paint
the lily."  Are not these tales their own best inter-
preter?  May not our clumsy words only obscure
their worth?

And yet the very familiarity of the stories tends
to rob them of force.  To see them through
another's eyes may make them new again, even

though those eyes are all too dim for such a
task.

Let us, for convenience, think first of the lost
sheep and the lost coin, although it is impossible
not to realize all the time that the story of the lost
son is here also.

These stories are Jesus' defense of Himself for
keeping bad company. The publicans, Jews employed by Rome to collect the taxes, were not
unnaturally despised as being in Roman pay and
as helping to support Roman rule by the money
they raised. The very contact with Gentiles involved in their work was degrading in the eyes
of a strict Jew. The "sinners" were not only the
loose livers, but also those who were careless in
keeping the Jewish Law. The proper place for
a rabbi was discussing the Law and its application
with other rabbis, or teaching the respectable folk
in the synagogues. It was a positive scandal the
way this one ran about with these ne'er-do-wells,
who showed clearly by their lives that they had
no use for religion and no proper respect for its
ministers. One could not help suspecting that
there was something wrong with the teaching of a
man who could do such things.

The defense of Jesus was, in effect, that He
wanted to be where God was. Of course God
was with the sincere synagogue worshipers, but
He was also concerned about the publican and the
sinner—even more concerned, one might almost
say, because of the very fact that they had gone
astray. They belonged to God, but He had lost
them and He wanted them back. If He got even

one of them back, there was rejoicing in heaven. Jesus wanted to have a share in the divine search and the divine joy.

"This is not just an issue for theologians. Is there any shepherd here who has ever lost a sheep? He ought to be able to understand how God feels. Is there a woman here who has ever searched the house for a lost coin? She knows the thrill of finding. She can understand something of the heart of God. It is natural to search for lost property. Even God searches for what *He* has lost. You rabbis ought to be collaborating with God in seeking the lost, instead of criticizing." So Jesus argues.

When we read the word "lost" in the New Testament or hear it in church, we are apt to think of "lost souls," of the Last Judgment and of hell. Without pausing to discuss the reality of such thoughts, it must be urged that we shall never understand these stories unless we take them naturally. A thing is "lost" when its owner is deprived of the proper use and enjoyment of it. A coin is lost when it cannot be used as coinage or an ornament. A sheep is lost when it has strayed away from the care and control of its shepherd. A son is lost when he wanders away from the knowledge and fellowship of his parents. We shall probably wish to be much more cautious than our forefathers in dogmatizing about what "damnation" is and the fate of the "damned." At any rate we ought to recognize in these stories when Jesus talks by analogy of men being "lost" to God what He means is that they are lost to the divine service and fellowship; they are not in their proper place, or fulfilling their true end in life of serving God and enjoying Him forever. To say this is not to belittle the tragedy of the wasted life; it is to try to bring reality into the discussion and to argue as Jesus did from the known to the unknown. "Lost" here cannot be translated "damned." Indeed, the great point of the stories is that the situation is not hopeless. The sheep is away from the fold where it belongs; the coin is out of use; the boy is away from the home that is waiting for him. But they can be brought back. And they are.

It matters to God that one man should waste his life. Someone cherished and serviceable is missing from the divine family if everybody is not within the circle. The home is not happy while there is a vacant place. God does not just love "mankind." He cares for us one by one. It is no real consolation to the shepherd to tell him that he has still got ninety-nine left. He wants the one that is not there. For the shepherd the most important sheep for the time being is the one that needs him most. So it is with God. Jesus is not suggesting that God does not love those that never get lost. When the shepherd leaves the flock "in the wilderness," he is not being careless, as the words might suggest. The wilderness is just the uncultivated pasture ground where the sheep ought to be.

There is perhaps more than a touch of irony in Jesus' reference to the "just persons who seek no repentance." Perhaps the Pharisee was just as lost as the publican if he only knew it.  Jesus has pictured in another story the Pharisee who thought he needed no repentance; and He tells us what God thought about *him*.

It has, however, been argued that the one sheep represents the human race as a whole, not particularly wayward individuals.  Plummer, in his commentary on Luke, says that Cyril of Alexandria and Ambrose regard the straying sheep as mankind and the ninety and nine as the angels.[1]  "Jesus is not comparing flagrant sinners with very hypothetical righteous, but is depicting mankind as a whole, the one straying and sinful being in all God's world, who is yet dearer to Him than others, and over whose retrieval He rejoices more, than over the blameless beauties and joys of lives not capable of sin."[2]

It does not seem possible to be sure whether the coin (worth about sixteen cents) was part of the treasured savings of a poor household, or part of a circlet worn round the head, perhaps a bridal ornament and therefore valued as we here value a wedding ring.  In either case the picture is a vivid one.  The little house is built to keep out the hot sun, but that inevitably means keeping out the daylight also.  So the lamp is needed (Mark 4. 21) when anything small is to be found in a corner.  It is a poor affair at best, this wick floating in a kind of saucer of clay; it is not normally meant for working by.  But the lamp

---

[1] *International Critical Commentary,* p. 368.
[2] A. T. Cadoux, *The Parables of Jesus,* p. 232.

and the vigorously applied broom at last succeed, and the woman runs out of the cottage, coin in hand, to tell the whole story to the neighbors.

How daring of Jesus to say that heaven was like that! The peasant woman laughing with the neighbors, the shepherd telling his cronies the story of how he got his sheep back, are pictures of the angels of heaven rejoicing together over a sinful man won back to fellowship with God.

"There is joy in the presence of the Place"—the divine dwelling place—"when those who provoke Him to anger disappear from the world." So said Rabbi Ishmael ben Elisha about the year 110 A. D.[3] But Jesus said, "There is joy in the presence of the angels of God over one sinner that repenteth."

---

[3] Dalman, *The Words of Jesus,* p. 210.

# XVII

## THE PRODIGAL SON

He also said: "There was a man who had two sons, and the younger said to his father, 'Father, give me the share of the property that falls to me.' So he divided his means among them. Not many days later, the younger son sold off everything and went abroad to a distant land, where he squandered his means in loose living. After he had spent his all, a severe famine set in throughout that land, and he began to feel in want; so he went and attached himself to a citizen of that land, who sent him to his fields to feed swine. And he was fain to fill his belly with the pods the swine were eating; no one gave him anything. But when he came to his senses he said, 'How many hired men of my father have more than enough to eat, and here am I perishing of hunger! I will be up and off to my father, and I will say to him, "Father, I have sinned against heaven and before you; I don't deserve to be called your son any more; only make me like one of your hired men."' So he got up and went off to his father. But when he was still far away his father saw him and felt pity for him and ran to fall upon his neck and kiss him. The son said to him, 'Father, I have sinned against heaven and before you; I don't deserve to be called your son any more.' But the father said to his servants, 'Quick, bring the best robe and put it on him, give him a ring for his hand and sandals for his feet, and bring the fatted calf, kill it, and let us eat and be merry; for my son here was dead and he has come to life, he was lost and he is found.' So they began to make merry. Now his elder son was out in the field, and as he came near the house he heard music

165

and dancing; so, summoning one of the servants, he asked what this meant. The servant told him, 'Your brother has arrived, and your father has killed the fatted calf because he has got him back safe and sound.' This angered him, and he would not go in. His father came out and tried to appease him, but he replied, 'Look at all the years I have been serving you! I have never neglected any of your orders, and yet you have never given me so much as a kid, to let me make merry with my friends. But as soon as this son of yours arrives, after having wasted your means with harlots, you kill the fatted calf for him!' The father said to him, 'My son, you and I are always together, all I have is yours. We could not but make merry and rejoice, for your brother here was dead and has come to life again, he was lost but he has been found.' "— *Luke* 15. 11-32.

IT is an impressive fact that Jesus used illustrations drawn from the home for His profoundest teaching. He told us that the nature of the Creator and Sustainer of the universe was more like the loving heart of a father than anything else we could imagine. If men wanted to know what God was like, they were to think of the best possible human fatherhood, and then believe that God is infinitely better still. Fatherhood, according to Jesus, is our best clue to the character of God. The apostle Paul expresses the same thought the other way round, as it were. He says that every fatherhood on earth derives its name and nature from the divine Fatherhood.

It is true of most of us not only that we first begin to appreciate the love of our fathers and mothers when we have children of our own, but also few events in life have so profound a reli-

gious influence upon us as the birth and nurture of
a child.   Through our fatherhood and motherhood
we learn something about our Father in heaven.

Jesus tells us too that the kingdom of God,
the community over which God rules in reality,
will be a great family of men and women living as
brothers and sisters worthily of their Father.   So
that the home in the thought of Jesus is woven
into the eternal structure of the universe.

This is nowhere illustrated more movingly than
here.   If in the story of the lost sheep our Lord
appeals to the experience of any shepherd, in this
story He appeals to fathers and mothers.   "It
would not be an undue stretch of imagination to
picture among those hoary-headed Pharisees and
scribes, who listened to our Lord's words, one or
another to whom they appealed personally with
painful interest."[1]   To allegorize is to miss the
point.   To say the father in the parable is God,
or even symbolizes God, is to be involved in
difficulties of interpretation.   The story cannot
be made to fit.   For example, God did not wait
at home for the prodigal human race to return.
Jesus, rather, says: "Here is a tale of how a good
father treated an erring son—or, rather, two erring
sons.   God's attitude toward men is rather like that.
This is the best picture I can draw in human terms
of the love of God."

The chief character in the story is not the
prodigal son; it is the prodigal's father.   It might
be entitled "The Parable of the Good Father."

---

[1] Oesterley, p. 185.

The real pathos of the story is not in the suffering of the prodigal; it is in the sorrow of the lonely father, who every now and again found himself looking at the place where the figure of his son had disappeared from his sight. Until one day— marvelous to relate—he reappeared, sadly altered but still recognizable even a great way off by a father's eye. And the father runs—yes, actually runs[2]—to meet him, and in his joy stifles at their birth all the son's carefully rehearsed speeches of apology. The son perhaps forgot the father while he was in the far country, perhaps ceased to love him in any real way. But he could not destroy his father's love for him. It was there waiting all the while. And perhaps when he got home he realized something of what he had been doing. No doubt he had stoutly asserted many a time that it was his own life he was living, and that he was prepared to take the consequences. Now he knew that there were consequences he could not bear for himself. His father had been wounded for his transgressions and bruised for his iniquities.

Our Lord exhausts the resources of language to bring home to men His stupendous doctrine of the love of God. "Are not five sparrows sold for two farthings? And not one of them is forgotten in the sight of God. But the very hairs of your head are numbered. Fear not: ye are of more value than many sparrows." God cares for each man in the way this father cared about the prodi- gal. Incredible! Yet that is what Jesus says.

---

[2] Aristotle says that great-souled men will never run in public.

There is a home for any of us, and a welcome with
God.   God's love for us has its reasons in itself,
not in our deservings.   His love beareth all things,
believeth all things, hopeth all things, endureth all
things, and never faileth.

The sheep strayed unwittingly, blindly; the
coin was not to blame for getting lost.   But the
going of the boy was willful.   The shepherd
followed the sheep and brought it back.   The
woman searched with lamp and broom and picked
up the coin.   But when the son went, the father
did not follow.   A forcible bringing home of
the body when the heart was away would have
achieved little.   The son who chose to go must
choose to return.

But the father had allies in memory and conscience and the experience of life.   The far
country was more attractive at a distance than in
reality.   The son did not belong there.   "When
he came to himself," when he got his senses back,
he realized what a fool he had been.   He had
been "beside himself" to leave home like that.
No doubt the thought of his father's well-stocked
table had a good deal to do with his change of
attitude.   Feeding pigs was in itself a degrading
occupation for a Jew; he must have sunk pretty
low to accept it.   The pittance he earned as a
swineherd could not cope with famine prices.
He would like to have taken his share in the
troughs with his swine.[3]   It was not till he was

---

[3] Mr. Levison (*The Parables: Their Background and Local
Setting,* p. 157) points out that as the prodigal could not help
himself, the food in question does not mean the food in the

in a state of complete destitution that he thought
of returning home. He was "down and out," a
badly paid, underfed pagan drudge.

Yet it was more than the hope of a good meal
that drew him. We need not suspect his prepared
speech as insincere, and it betrays at least the
consciousness that he has treated his father badly.
He was thoroughly ashamed of himself. "I have
sinned against heaven and in thy sight and am no
more worthy to be called thy son." He knew he
deserved nothing and yet he had confidence in his
father's kindness. He would surely not be turned
away. It would be good to be back even as a hired
servant.

But his father was beyond all counting better
than his hopes. He was on the lookout. The
impatience of love overcame his Eastern dignity.
He ran to meet the returning prodigal, and had
reinstated him as a son before the boy could get
the words of his speech out of his mouth. Everything was forgotten, except the joy that the son was
home again.

Mr. H. G. Wood says,[4] with reference to this
parable: "A well-known story of a returning
prodigal in Buddhist sources depicts a father
acting with proper caution under the circumstances. The father hides from the son, and puts

pasture, but, rather, the food given to the pigs on their return
from the field. There is an oval-shaped nut called *egoz chazir*
in modern Hebrew, which tastes like a chestnut, and is used for
food for goats and sheep and swine, the very name of it is "swine
nut." It is used as human food only by the very poor. Mr.
Levison believes that it is this nut which is referred to in the
parable.

[4] *Christianity and the Nature of History*, p. 71.

him to a series of tests until the genuineness of
his conversion permits his full restoration. To
many this form of the story will seem much more
rational and sensible, as indeed it is. But then in
Luke 15 there are expressed a life and thought
out of the ordinary. Behind it and through it we
see a conviction of God's love, not without
parallel perhaps, but seldom if ever expressed with
such clear and convincing power. The story was
never copied from some commonplace book. It
springs from life, the life that is always felt through
the teaching of Jesus when men are great enough
or simple enough to open their minds to it.

"The father said to his servants, Bring forth the
best robe and put it on him; and put a ring on
his hand, and shoes on his feet; and bring hither
the fatted calf and kill it; and let us eat and be
merry; for this my son was dead and is alive
again; he was lost and is found. And they began
to be merry."

Here at first sight seems the true climax. Why
spoil this by the somber anticlimax of the rest?

In the story of the prodigal brother our Lord
provides a mirror for his critics. The tale is not
complete without the two sons, "the self-righteous
prig" as well as "the silly wastrel."[5] For the prig
was lost too, though he had kept all the commandments.

Rudyard Kipling has suggested that the elder
brother provided one reason at least why the
younger left home. There is something very un-

---

[5] Herbert Gray, *The Christian Adventure,* p. 75.

lovely about him—jealousy, self-righteousness,
sulkiness all speak in his complaint. Jesus would
have us rearrange our list of virtues and vices. He
does not make light of the vices of the prodigal,
disgusting in themselves and the cause of suffering
to others. But He does suggest that perhaps the
elder brother was just as bad with his spirit of
hard self-righteousness, doing his duty for the sake
of reward, respectable, but selfish and cruel. And
He meant His critics to see if the cap fitted.

But that was not all He had to say to the critics.
There is forgiveness for these sins too, and the
elder brother is also "my boy." (The word
translated "son" in verse 31 is an affectionate
form.) "My boy, thou art ever with me and all
that I have is thine." It is a most kindly reply
to a churlish complaint. The Pharisee also is
God's child, and the Father's home stands open
for him too.

"This man receiveth sinners and eateth with
them!" Surely, replied Jesus to the critics, it is
meet that we should make merry and be glad. For
these your brothers were dead and are alive again.
They were lost and are found.

The story of the prodigal is a wonderful story.
But John Baillie has written some very wise words
about it. "When Jesus wished to make manifest
to men the redemptive love of God, He invented
the story of the prodigal son, and it is, I suppose,
the most beautiful story that has ever been invented by anybody. Yet we must not forget that
behind the story told, and giving reality and conviction to the telling of it, there was the character

and the life of the Teller. . . . In truth, there is
for us another story that is more wonderful still, a
story stranger and more beautiful than any fiction,
and yet one which Jesus Himself could not fully
tell, because the first chapters of it were only being
enacted as He spoke.  But when a few years afterward Peter and Paul and John went about in their
turn to prove that same redemptive love of God
to the men of their own day, they were able to
preach to them a better sermon and to announce
to them a fuller Christianity than even the Master
Himself had been able to do; for instead of telling
them the parable of the prodigal son, they could
now tell them the history of the Passion of
Christ."[6]

---

[6] *The Roots of Religion,* pp. 201-203.

# XVIII

## THE UNJUST STEWARD

He also said to the disciples: "There was a rich man who had a factor, and this factor, he found, was accused of misapplying his property. So he summoned him and said, 'What is this I hear about you? Hand in your accounts; you cannot be factor any longer.' The factor said to himself, 'What am I to do now that my master is taking the factorship away from me? I am too weak to dig, I am ashamed to beg. Ah, I know what I will do, so that people will welcome me to their houses when I am deposed from the factorship.' So he summoned every single one of his master's debtors. He asked the first, 'How much are you owing to my master?' 'A hundred barrels of oil,' he said. The factor told him, 'Here is your bill; sit down at once and enter fifty barrels.' Then he asked another, 'And how much do you owe?' 'A hundred quarters of wheat,' he said. 'Here is your bill,' said the factor, 'just enter eighty.' Well, the master praised the dishonest factor for looking ahead; for the children of this world look further ahead in dealing with their own generation than the children of Light. And I tell you, use mammon, dishonest as it is, to make friends for yourselves, so that when you die they may welcome you to the eternal abodes.

"He who is faithful with a trifle is also faithful with
    a large trust,
    and he who is dishonest with a trifle is also dis-
      honest with a large trust.
So if you are not faithful with dishonest mammon,
    how can you ever be trusted with true Riches?

And if you are not faithful with what belongs to
    another,
  how can you ever be given what is your own?
No servant can serve two masters:
    either he will hate the one and love the other,
    or else he will stand by the one and despise the
      other—
you cannot serve both God and Mammon."
                —*Luke* 16. 1-13.

THIS parable has occasioned a great deal of
perplexity, and it is certainly surprising, on
the face of it, to find our Lord commending the
actions of an unprincipled scoundrel as a model
of good behavior.

This man abused his responsibility as adminis-
trator of his master's affairs. He was found out
and faced by ruin. He then extricates himself from
disaster by putting his master's debtors under obligation to himself by "cooking the accounts" so as
to reduce their indebtedness considerably.[1] When
his dismissal took effect, he could count on their
hospitality and support—under threat of black-
mail if not willingly. When his master discovered this further robbery, the sheer audacity and
cleverness of the man compelled a certain admiration.

So far all seems clear enough. But why did
Jesus use this unscrupulous blackguard as an
example? Our trouble about the story and the

---

[1] Levison, *op. cit.,* p. 166, comments on this part of the story:
"Borrowing was, and is, very common in Palestine, and a debt is
seldom paid in money, but almost always in produce from the
farm." Possibly, however, they were tenants paying rent in
kind.

comments on it is largely due to our insistence upon allegorizing the parable and seeking spiritual counterparts for all the characters.  Once we are clear that this is a plain story of rascality and not an allegory, things become easier.  The "lord" of the steward is not intended to represent God.  The employer is just a cynical man of the world who appreciates the astuteness of the rogue, though it is to his own disadvantage.  It is the kind of approval that one might express for a burglar's cleverness in getting the safe open, or for the skill of a forger who imitates a banknote.

It seems probable that "the lord" of verse 8 (R. V., *his* lord) does not refer to Jesus.  The story ends at the middle of the verse, and the comments of Jesus upon it begin with the second half: "For the sons of this world are for their own generation wiser than the sons of light."   In other words, "Why do you let yourselves be outdone by the world in keenness and foresight?"

These people live up to their own principles (or lack of them) and carry them through with thoroughness.  The skill and daring of the wicked in doing evil ought to be emulated by the Christian in doing good.  One might carry the argument a stage further and urge Christians not only to be as keen as other people, but even to apply to the service of God the same devotion and skill as they themselves give to the advancement of their own interests.  It is not only that people apply themselves with more thoroughness to their business and professional careers than to their religious discipleship.  They will devote more time and money and energy to reducing their golf handicap or to mastering a tennis stroke or to growing roses, that is, to their leisure pursuits and amusements, than they will to the service and support of the cause of Christ. How languid Christians can be in their Christianity!

It is not clear, however, how far the following verses are really connected with the parable. Verse 9 seems clearly to belong, but verses 10-13 seem to be very loosely linked with the story, if at all. Perhaps the connecting link of the verses is the references to Mammon,[2] which led to the putting together of what were originally independent sayings.

It is possible that three separate "morals" (no doubt all sayings of Jesus, but spoken in different contexts) were attached to this parable because the evangelist was himself puzzled as to the true application of the story. (1) The children of this world are for their own generation wiser than the sons of light. (2) Make yourselves friends by means of the mammon of unrighteousness. (3) If you are not faithful in the unrighteous mammon, who will trust you with true riches?

The exact meaning of the phrase "the mammon of unrighteousness" is difficult to determine. It might mean wealth unrighteously acquired. P. N. F. Young, in *The College Saint Luke* (p. 322), suggests that "the saying may be out of its context, and have been addressed to a group of tax-gatherers, and it would then be equivalent to:

---

[2] Mammon is just a personification of money; the actual derivation of the word is uncertain.

'You have made money dishonestly, but if now you use your wealth in works of charity and beneficence, it may stand you in good stead where a better kind of wealth is the currency' " (compare the story of Zacchaeus, Luke 19. 1-10). It may, however, mean "wealth to which the unrighteous trust." Faithfulness in handling money will qualify for the possession of spiritual riches. Make provision in this life for the next world, as the unjust steward made provision for his future.

Taken as isolated sayings the verses are pregnant with meaning, but not difficult to understand. The difficulty of interpretation is almost entirely due to the effort, probably needless, to connect them with one another and with the parable. It is best to regard them as a cluster of sayings about the use and abuse of wealth.

# XIX

## DIVES AND LAZARUS

There was a rich man, clad in purple and fine linen, who lived sumptuously every day. Outside his door lay a poor man called Lazarus; he was a mass of ulcers, and fain to eat up the crumbs that fell from the rich man's table. (The very dogs used to come and lick his ulcers.) Now it happened that the poor man died, and he was carried by the angels to Abraham's bosom. The rich man died too, and was buried. And as he was being tortured in Hades he raised his eyes and saw Abraham far away with Lazarus in his bosom; so he called out, "Father Abraham, take pity on me, send Lazarus to dip his fingertip in water and cool my tongue, for I am in anguish in these flames." But Abraham said, "Remember, my son, you got all the bliss when you were alive, just as Lazarus got the ills of life; he is in comfort now, and you are in anguish. Besides all that, a great gulf yawns between us and you, to keep back those who want to cross from us to you and also those who want to pass from you to us." Then he said, "Well, father, I beg you to send him to my father's house, for I have five brothers; let him bear testimony to them, that they may not come to this place of torture as well." "They have got Moses and the prophets," said Abraham, "they can listen to them." "No, father Abraham," he said, "but if some-one only goes to them from the dead, they will repent." He said to him, "If they will not listen to Moses and the prophets, they will not be convinced, not even if one rose from the dead."—*Luke* 16. 19-31.

THERE are three acts in the "Tragedy of the Selfish Rich Man." The two chief characters are the Rich Man himself, whom we may conveniently call Dives, which is, of course, just the Latin for "rich man," and Lazarus, the beggar. The latter is the only character in a parable to whom our Lord has given a personal name. It would seem that there must be some significance in this, but it is hard to be sure what it is. The name, of Hebrew derivation, means "God is my helper," or "He whom God helps." Is it intended to suggest the religious faith of the beggar? Or that God cares for him though man neglects him, as the story shows?

## ACT I

The scene is the home of Dives. He is a wealthy man of the world and a respectable pillar of society. He could afford the most luxurious clothing and the most sumptuous meals, and he indulged his fancies. And why not? No charge is made against his character or the means by which he earned his money. He is just a rich man who likes to be comfortable, and surely his spending is "good for trade."

At his gate lies Lazarus, the beggar, a mass of sores, ill clad and hungry. He catches sight at times of the banqueting within the house, and longs for a share of even the crumbs from the table. From time to time the servants throw out the leavings into the streets and he manages to get some, but his claims are disputed by the dogs at their

usual task of scavenging.[1]  It adds to his misery
that he cannot keep off these mangy snarling brutes.
Dogs in the East are not the pets and friends of
man, but unwelcome pests.

Lazarus presents as notable a figure of poverty
and misery as Dives does of luxury.  He is a familiar
figure lying there at the gate, and Dives often sees
him as he passes in and out.

There is no caricature in the picture, no bitterness, or "class feeling."  It is just a plain statement
of fact—a poor man at a rich man's gates.

## ACT II

The scene is the next world.  Hades is described
in terms of popular Jewish conceptions.  Our Lord
is not here teaching His hearers about the conditions of the next life.  His concern is elsewhere.
Hades is not "hell" as we use the term today; it is
the place where all men go at death.  "Paradise"
and "Gehenna" are two parts of it, within sight and
hearing of each other, but separated.

Dives and Lazarus have died.  Dives, we are told,
was buried.  His funeral was worthy of mention,
celebrated with all proper pomp.  There were
plenty of hired mourners and purchased tears, however many real ones there may have been.  The
burial of Lazarus is not mentioned.  Probably few
noted the passage of the emaciated frame to a

---

[1] Montefiore points out that "crumbs" is misleading: "What
fell from the table were big bits of bread which were used to
clean or dry the hands after the eaters had dipped them, for
example, in a dish full of bits of meat and gravy.  Napkins were
not used for the hands."—*Synoptic Gospels*, ii. 1003.

pauper's grave.  But we are told that his soul had an escort of angels to the next world.

If the setting of the scene is on conventional lines, the disposition of the personnel is startling.

Abraham, the father of the faithful, is presiding at a feast.  Reclining on the couch next to him, in the place of honor, is the one-time beggar, Lazarus. Here is astonishment enough.  But a voice breaks the silence.  It comes from Dives in torment, begging for a drop of water!  From his place in Gehenna he has caught sight of Lazarus and hastens to claim acquaintance.  It is Lazarus who is rich now and Dives who is in dire want.

Here, at any rate, is poetic justice.  As Abraham reminds Dives, he had his share of good things on earth.  Now it is the turn of Lazarus.  No other reason is given for the strange reversal of fortune.

Dives is sure there is some mistake.  Is he not an Israelite?  Is not Abraham his father?  He can surely appeal to him with confidence.  He would be grateful for the least alleviation of his torment.

But Abraham, though he admits the relationship, can do nothing for his "son."  The gulf that separated Dives and Lazarus on earth is still there in the next world.  And now it is impassable and eternal.

## Act III

The scene is the same.  Dives has apparently accepted the inevitability if not the justice of his own position.  He now pleads for others, his five brothers at home in grave danger of sharing his fate unless something is done to warn them.

Some writers have seen in his concern for others the dawning of a better spirit in the soul of Dives. King Lear, deserted by his daughters, and exposed for the first time unprotected to the fury of the elements, begins to have a new sympathy for his poverty-stricken subjects:

> "Poor naked wretches, wheresoe'er you are,
>   That bide the pelting of this pitiless storm,
>   How shall your houseless heads and unfed sides,
>   Your loop'd and window'd raggedness, defend you
> From seasons such as these? O! I have ta'en
> Too little care of this! Take physic, pomp;
> Expose thyself to feel what wretches feel,
> That thou may'st shake the superflux to them
> And show the heavens more just."[2]

So concern for others wakens in the heart of Dives. However that may be, there is more than a suspicion of self-justification in the plea. The plea "is not so much an ebbing of selfishness as an attempt to justify selfishness. He implies that his brothers were living under a handicap: they had not been properly warned."[3] Why was *I* never told? he seems to say. I never realized the risk I was running. Is it fair to punish men so without warning them?

Abraham is not moved. Men have all the warning they need. People ought to be humane from motives of humanity, not because of threats or bribes. "If they can be inhuman with the Bible in their hands and Lazarus at their gate, no reve-

[2] *King Lear*, Act iii, Scene 4.
[3] Buttrick, *The Parables of Jesus*, p. 144.

lation of the splendors of heaven or the anguish of hell will ever make them anything else."[4]

The sting of the parable, someone has said, lies in its reference to the five brothers, behaving as Dives did and in peril of a like end. Who were the brothers? Surely, just those to whom Jesus was speaking—and, perhaps, you and me. What has it to say to us?

Our Lord Himself added no comment or explanation to the story—at least none has been recorded. But though no judgment on the characters is recorded in a formal way, yet there is revealed in the story what Dale called "the indignation of infinite love at white heat." Alexander Maclaren calls this "the sternest of Christ's parables."

It is clear that to Jesus such a life as that of Dives is profoundly immoral, highly respectable and customary as it may be. It has sometimes been complained that Dives did nothing for which he could be blamed. That is just the point. Dives is condemned precisely because he did nothing. A wealthy man has a beggar at his gate and nothing is done. Such selfish living is to Jesus a deadly sin. Here is a man of privilege who is unfit to have it.

Is this parable an attack on the wealthy and a defense of the poor? Is Jesus an advocate of the class struggle? This parable can hardly be taken as a condemnation of all rich men, or wealthy

[4] Denney, *The Way Everlasting*, p. 171. The sermon, trenchant as is his wont, is well worth studying.

Abraham would not be presiding at the feast. It is, rather, an attack on the misuse of riches. Yet are not such extremes of poverty and wealth as Lazarus and Dives represent, in themselves immoral and utterly unjustifiable? Can we make any protest if heaven reverses the situation and fills the hungry with good things while it sends the rich empty away? Doubtless the fine linen and champagne of Dives are as little deserved as the rags of Lazarus. "You've had your turn, Dives. Now it is the turn of Lazarus."

But, of course, our Lord is probing deeper than that.

Selfish wealth while there exists abject poverty is itself an evil. It denies brotherhood. It shrinks the soul of rich and poor alike. It digs a gulf between men. On earth Dives had carefully insulated himself from Lazarus as far as he could. Even if he had tried to make friends with Lazarus, the difference in their positions would have made true friendship impossible. Even wealth well used digs a gulf. We need not believe that Christianity demands equality of income to hold strongly that no Christian ought to acquiesce in an order of society which permits such extremes of undeserved wealth and poverty as we find today in America and Great Britain, to go no farther afield.

Dives just took the social order for granted. He was probably not especially inhuman. He was callous about the needs he saw every day, but it probably never occurred to him that they were any responsibility of his. He didn't really *see* Lazarus. He just took him for granted as a part

of the street scene.   And it is terribly easy for any
one of us to do the same.

For the gulf between the comfortable and the
poor in modern life means that they never
meet.   Most of those who read this book belong
to the comfortable classes.   We probably do not
live in the depressed areas.   Even in our own town
or city we are not confronted by the undernour-
ished, the disappointed, the distressed, the diseased.
We live in the suburbs.   The really poor are segre-
gated by themselves.   We probably have few real
friends among them.   "The unemployed" so easily
become figures read to us over the radio once a
month. . . . And it is comforting to know that
there are fewer millions than there were.

Of the wretchedness that modern society hides
away in hospital and home, poorhouse and asylum
and prison, we probably know even less.   One of
the startling revelations of a visit to the East is
to see wandering about in the streets of town or
village hideously maimed and deformed figures
such as the ordinary man never sees in America—
not because they do not exist, but because they
are hidden from us.

Let this parable say to us now, not in the next
world, "Son, remember, that thou receivest good
things and Lazarus evil things."   Let us try by
concern, by friendship, by personal service, as
opportunity offers, by working and voting for a
better order of society even though to our own
hurt, to fill in the "great gulf."   Let us shut our
ears to "all the easy speeches that comfort cruel
men."   "If there is no child labor," they said a

century ago, "then the cotton industry must perish." "Better let the cotton industry perish," cried Carlyle, "than be built upon the rickety bodies of ill-fed children."

In the mind of Luke this parable is clearly connected with the preceding verses 14 and 15, and may, of course, have actually been spoken at the same time. It is a rebuke to the scoffing Pharisees who were "lovers of money." It might well be a sermon on the text: "That which is exalted among men is an abomination in the sight of God."

The parable might be regarded also as emphasizing the fact that this life is the decisive arena of moral judgment. The sayings of our Lord about the next life "never traverse the principle that this life is the scene of opportunity and this world the theater of human fates."[5] We may speculate as to whether men get "a second chance" in the next world, and perhaps a good case can be made out on general principles, but we cannot quote any sayings of Jesus to endorse it. Certainly, to discuss this story as an exposition of the nature of the future life is to miss the point. We cannot build doctrine on its details. The parable is a lesson about humanity in this world, not a lesson about conditions in the next world. Inhumanity shuts a man out of heaven (compare Matthew 25. 31-46).

Men have light enough to guide them. They have Moses and the prophets (verse 29) and

---

[5] Salmond, *The Christian Doctrine of Immortality*, p. 392.

Lazarus.    Speculations about the nature of the future life may easily be futile, and fuller knowledge of its nature would not necessarily lead to more noble living in this world.    A more urgent question, suggests Jesus, is: What have you done with Lazarus at your gate?

## XX

## UNPROFITABLE SERVANTS

Which of you, with a servant out plowing or shepherding, will say to him when he comes in from the field, "Come at once and take your place at table"? Will the man not rather say to him, "Get something ready for my supper; gird yourself and wait on me till I eat and drink; then you can eat and drink yourself"? Does he thank the servant for doing his bidding? Well, it is the same with you; when you have done all you are bidden, say, "We are but servants;[1] we have only done our duty."—*Luke* 17. 7-10.

WE can never make God our debtor. We can never say: We have done more in His service than could reasonably be expected of us. We owe everything to God—as Creator, Father, Redeemer. We owe Him life itself, our bodies and our minds. By the most arduous self-cultivation we can do no more than develop our innate God-given capacities. And He has sustained us, redeemed us, forgiven us. If we catch even a glimpse of the greatness of His love in Christ to such as we are—of His "grace," as the New Testament calls it, His free, unmerited bounty—we

---

[1] Omitting ἀχρεῖοι with Syr.[sin.] followed by most recent editors. The emphasis falls on the simple fact of being slaves, not on any distinction between good and bad slaves.

189

can only confess, "We never deserved *that* and we can never repay it." We have obligations but no claim to reward.

> "For merit lives from man to man,
>     And not from man, O God, to Thee."

Our proper status in relation to God is that of servants. It is His to command and ours to obey. One of the manuscripts omits the word "unprofitable," and a number of scholars agree that it may well be an interpolation. In any case the stress lies upon the position of the servants, not on the quality of their service. "We are servants. We have done our duty."

It seems possible that this parable was called forth by request of the sons of Zebedee for special privilege in the kingdom of God (Matthew 20. 20-28; Mark 10. 35-45). This incident is not recorded by Luke, though he does report sayings which Matthew and Mark connect with it. (See Luke 22. 25-27.)

"Christ would have His disciples understand that the Christian vocation is a very high one indeed; that for those who give themselves to it, it not merely brings hard toil in the fields through the day, but also, so to speak, extra duties in the evening, when the weary laborer would fain be at rest; that it has no fixed hours of labor—eight, ten, twelve, as the case may be, according to agreement—but may summon to work at any hour of all the twenty-four, as in the case of soldiers in time of war, or of farm laborers in the season of harvest, when the grain must be secured when weather is propitious."[2]

There are times when we are tempted to escape our duty or evade our responsibilities. Our tasks wear unlovely faces. We feel we are being called upon to do more than is fair and reasonable. But there is no mistake about it; God does claim our all. The rich young ruler asserted, and probably sincerely, that he had kept the letter of the Law. He had done his duty. What more could be expected? "Sell what thou hast and give to the poor," said Jesus. That particular command was not for all disciples; it was addressed to the individual. But what was lacking in him is lacking in many of us. He had not the spirit of abandon to the cause of Christ. He was dutiful, but not enthusiastic. He was not ready to give himself unreservedly.

The great saints found their joy in so giving themselves. The call of service is willingly and swiftly obeyed. With the psalmist they cry, "I delight to do thy will."

"If you knew," said David Livingstone to the undergraduates of Cambridge, "the satisfaction of performing such a duty, as well as the gratitude to God which the missionary must always feel in being chosen for so noble, so sacred a calling, you would have no hesitation in embracing it.

"For my own part I have never ceased to rejoice that God has appointed me to such an office. People talk of the sacrifice I have made in spend-

---

[2] Bruce, *Parabolic Teaching*, p. 172.

ing so much of my life in Africa.  Can that be
called a sacrifice which is simply paid back as
a small part of a great debt owing to our God
which we can never repay?  Is that a sacrifice
which brings its own blest reward in healthful
activity, the consciousness of doing good, peace
of mind, and a bright hope of a glorious resting
hereafter? . . . It is emphatically no sacrifice.  Say,
rather, it is a privilege.  Anxiety, sickness, suffering or danger, now and then, with a foregoing of
the common conveniences and charities of this life,
may make us pause and cause the spirit to waver
and the soul to sink; but let this only be for a
moment. . . . I never made a sacrifice.  Of this we
ought not to talk when we remember the great
sacrifice which He made who left His Father's
throne on high to give Himself for us."[3]

It makes all the difference to realize that the
obligation is not to an abstract law, but to a Person
who is worthy of the utmost we can give; and
one who, in fact, has treated us vastly differently
from this Taskmaster of the parable.  Slaveowners
did commonly behave so, and we should have no
cause to grumble if that were the attitude of
almighty God.  But the point is our attitude toward
God and not how God treats us.  He might
justly so treat us, but in reality: "Blessed are
those servants whom the lord when he cometh shall
find watching: verily I say unto you, that he shall
gird himself, and make them sit down to meat,
and shall come and serve them" (Luke 12. 37).  He

---

[3] *The Life of David Livingstone*, W. G. Blaikie, p. 190.

no longer calls us servants, but friends (see John
15. 15).

If we once realize the real situation, what we
are and what God is, we shall be sure we can never
do enough.  The measure of our duty will be seen
to be the measure of our opportunities.  "Enlarge
our hearts," will be our prayer, "that we may *run*
the way of thy commandments."  To be satisfied
with our service of God is spiritual death.

# XXI

## THE PHARISEE AND THE PUBLICAN

He also told the following parable to certain persons who were sure of their own goodness and looked down upon everybody else. "Two men went up to pray in the temple; one was a Pharisee and the other was a taxgatherer. The Pharisee stood up and prayed by himself as follows: 'I thank thee, O God, I am not like the rest of men, thieves, rogues, and immoral, or even like yon taxgatherer. Twice a week I fast; on all my income I pay tithes.' But the taxgatherer stood far away and would not lift even his eyes to heaven, but beat his breast, saying, 'O God, have mercy on me for my sins!' I tell you, he went home accepted by God rather than the other man;

"for everyone who uplifts himself will be humbled,
　　and he who humbles himself will be uplifted."
　　　　　　　　　　　　　　　—*Luke* 18. 9-14.

"Two went to pray!　O rather say
　One went to brag—the other to pray:
　One stands up close and treads on high,
　Where the other dare not send his eye;
　One nearer to God's altar trod,
　The other to the altar's God."

　　　　　　　　　　　　　　　—*Crashaw*.

IT may be argued that this is not strictly a parable at all. It is not an incident drawn from nature or from human life to illustrate something else. It is not a parallel; it is an example of the truth under discussion, the peril of pride. It is noteworthy that Jesus selects as illustrative of the wrong attitude toward God a devout religious man, a thoroughly respectable member of society.    Was any critic of religion ever more severe than He was on its perversions?    Was there anything our Lord disliked more than unctuous piety?    It does not follow, of course, that He was implying that all Pharisees were like this one, any more than that all publicans were penitents.

The Pharisee came strutting into the presence of God "reeking with self-complacency,"[1] and almost struck an attitude as he took up his position for prayer.    The word used is an emphatic one —"standing erect."    (Standing, of course, was in itself a common attitude in prayer.)

He then proceeded to pray "with himself."    The phrase may mean no more than that he prayed silently, but in the context it suggests that his thoughts never got outside himself.    He was soliloquizing—congratulating himself upon an excellent record, casting an approving eye upon his charities and his pieties.    It was all a prayer of thanksgiving for his own achievements.    He has even gone beyond the requirements in tithing *all* his income and fasting twice in the week.    He has only to look at the slackness of other people to see how admirable was his own behavior.    Look at that publican over there, for example.    One really wonders how such as he dare to come to the Temple at all.

Everything, in short, is so satisfactory that there

[1] Alexander Maclaren.

is no need for petition. His prayer consists of statements. He was such a fine fellow that he could forgive himself. There was no need to ask for forgiveness from God.

The publican was very unobtrusive. A quiet corner was all he asked. Like, and yet how unlike the Pharisee, he felt that he stood in a class by himself. "God be merciful to me, *the* sinner." God would recognize him by that description, he felt. He had no excuses to offer. He could only cast himself upon the divine mercy.

There is no suggestion that the Pharisee was not speaking the truth. No doubt he did all he claimed. Nor need we question that the publican was a great sinner. Yet, as Bruce says, in the eyes of Christ "a man confessing sin is nearer to true goodness than a man boasting of his goodness."[2]

The Pharisee was perhaps right in his assertions, but he was altogether wrong in his heart and in his attitude both toward others and toward God. His was the sin of "the superior person"—pride and complacency.

Pride and self-sufficiency is the fundamental sin. Dante agrees with Thomas Aquinas in declaring it "the most grievous of all sins." It is present in any man who complacently compares himself with his fellows and preens himself upon his virtue. It shows itself in those who "compound for sins they are inclined to by damning those they have no mind to." Punctilious observance of ecclesiastical duties is no substitute for kindliness and humility.

---

[2] *Parabolic Teaching*, p. 319.

It is tempting at times to compare oneself with others, but what do we really know of the circumstances of others? What did the Pharisee really know about "this publican"? Sin is measured not only by quantity but by opportunity and the weight of temptation. To whom much is given, of him will much be required.

> "Who made the heart, 'tis He alone
>     Decidedly can try us;
> He knows each chord—its various tone,
>     Each spring—its various bias:
> Then at the balance let's be mute,
>     We never can adjust it;
> What's done we partly may compute,
>     But know not what's resisted."[3]

If the Pharisee had been meditating upon his privileges and the opportunities he enjoyed, he might fitly have said, "I am not as other men." But he was delighted not with what God had given him but with what he had done for God.

That was the root of his errors, his wrong attitude toward God. He thought of Him as a Taskmaster, and of religion as a profit-and-loss account in the Bank of Heaven. He was piling up an accumulation of "good deeds." He was blind to the true inwardness of religion—as an attitude of humble adoration, penitence, and childlike trust toward our Holy Father. No man who has seen God—or himself—can be satisfied in His presence. "Lord, if thou shouldst mark iniquity, O Lord, who should stand?" "If we say that we have no sin, we deceive

---

[3] Robert Burns, "Address to the Unco Guid, or the Rigidly Righteous."

ourselves and the truth is not in us." Even if the Pharisee were free from many varieties of sins, he was guilty of sin—the self-regarding, self-assertive attitude toward God, from which springs all sins.

The publican had nothing to be proud of. He believed in the mercy of God. And he received it. The publican went away "justified," in the Pauline sense of acceptance with God, not of high attainment of character. The publican did not necessarily *feel* justified as he left the Temple court. The point is what God thought of the publican, not what the publican felt. Probably the Pharisee went off with a greater sense of satisfaction than the publican. There is no more unreliable index of God's nearness or attitude toward us than our moods.

It is important to remember that God was quite as ready to forgive the Pharisee as He was to forgive the publican. The publican was "justified" not because he was a publican but because he repented. The Pharisee did not ask for forgiveness. It was there ready for him also, had he sought it.

## XXII

## THE LABORERS IN THE VINEYARD

For the Realm of heaven is like a householder who went out early in the morning to hire laborers for his vineyard; and after agreeing with the laborers to pay them a shilling a day he sent them into his vineyard. Then, on going out at nine o'clock he noticed some other laborers standing in the market-place doing nothing; to them he said, "You go into the vineyard too, and I will give you whatever wage is fair." So they went in. Going out again at twelve o'clock and at three o'clock, he did the same thing. And when he went out at five o'clock he came upon some others who were standing; he said to them, "Why have you stood doing nothing all the day?" "Because nobody hired us," they said. He told them, "You go into the vineyard too." Now when evening came the master of the vineyard said to his bailiff, "Summon the laborers and pay them their wages, beginning with the last and going on to the first." When those who had been hired about five o'clock came, they got a shilling each. So when the first laborers came up, they supposed they would get more; but they too got each their shilling. And on getting it they grumbled at the householder. "These last," they said, "have only worked a single hour, and yet you have ranked them equal to us who have borne the brunt of the day's work and the heat!" Then he replied to one of them, "My man, I am not wronging you. Did you not agree with me for a shilling? Take what belongs to you and be off. I choose to give this last man the same as you. Can I not do as

I please with what belongs to me? Have you a grudge because I am generous?" So shall the last be first and the first last.—*Matthew* 20. 1-16.

PETER evidently had an arithmetical mind. How many times was he to forgive? (Matthew 18. 18-22.)[1] He was prepared to be generous. He would suggest an outside number like seven times. But he did expect to be told definitely. And Jesus told him: "You are to forgive until seventy times seven, if you can keep count so long." In effect, our Lord said that you could not deal with such issues of personal relationships on a basis of regulations and rules.

So on another occasion he wanted to know how much recompense would be made to those who had given up everything in the service of Christ (Matthew 19. 27-30). The two sides of the equation must balance; so much service and sacrifice equals so much reward. Jesus replies sympathetically and assures Peter that certainly His servants are not without overflowing reward. Yet all the same Peter's question was wrong. It suggested a wrong attitude. The kingdom of God is not based upon rules of barter. Equal pay for equal work may be an entirely reasonable maxim in industry and commerce, but it does not apply to the service of God. We cannot

> "Make out and reckon on His ways,
>     And bargain for His love, and stand,
>         Paying a price, at His right hand."[2]

_____
[1] See p. 106.
[2] Browning, "Johannes Agricola."

We cannot be sure that the parable of the laborers in the vineyard was spoken by our Lord as part of His reply to this question from Peter. Perhaps it is set where it is in the Gospel merely by the plan of the editor. In either case the relevance of incident and parable to each other cannot be questioned.

Mr. Levison has an interesting paragraph which helps us to picture the setting of the story. "The grape-gathering season lasts from the beginning of August to the end of September. When the rainy season sets in about the end of September, every day, indeed every hour, is vitally important if the crop is to be gathered in safely. Thus the hire of laborers at a late hour is not at all unusual. The hiring of men at 6 and 9 A. M., noon, and 3 and 5 P. M. (Western time) is just what happens, but these men are paid according to the work done.[3]

"The owner in the case of our parable, however, acts with great generosity with the men who came to the vineyard at the late hour. He tells the paymaster to give each the same amount of pay. If we seek motives for this, two present themselves: (1) the fact that these men were not hired was no fault of theirs, and if they were paid just what was due, it would mean a supperless evening for the family. Out of the goodness of his heart, therefore, the owner gives full wages for the day. (2) It is

---

[3] It may be noted in passing that in the parable the day is reckoned from 6 A. M. till 6 P. M., so that "the eleventh hour," which has become with us proverbial for "the last minute," was in fact in its original meaning five o'clock in the afternoon. (Present writer's note.)

quite possible that the owner might reason that
the late-comers had saved him a great deal by
arriving just when they did and that they were
therefore worthy of full pay."[4]

Whatever the owner's motive, it not unnaturally
called forth a storm of protest from the other
workers who had "borne the burden and the heat
of the day." If the "penny" was a fair wage for
the late-comers, surely they deserved more.[5]

It has been suggested that if the motive were
merely generosity, he might have paid off the men
in the natural order. Those who had done a full
day's work would go off contented because they
had received the pay they had agreed upon. The
later ones would be proportionately grateful as
they got more than they had any right to expect,
but the earlier workers would by this time have
gone and no dispute need have arisen. The
reversal of the natural order seems to stress the
view of the owner that it was not right that men
willing to work should be without adequate main-
tenance.[6]

Neither here nor anywhere else was our Lord
speaking as a teacher of economics, and one has to
be cautious about transferring His sayings into the
realm of modern industry. But it is surely impossible to read this story without seeing that the
heart of the teller is moved at the spectacle of

---

[4] *The Parables: Their Background and Local Setting*, pp. 199-
200.

[5] The "penny," or denarius, was perhaps worth about nineteen
cents. Its purchasing power might be roughly equivalent to
about $1.20 in present-day terms.

[6] So A. T. Cadoux, *The Parables of Jesus*, p. 103.

unmerited unemployment. He is troubled to know that there are men standing idle in the market place because no man has hired them. Whatever be the "spiritual" application of the parable, that remains true. It is good to be reminded not that unemployment is no merely modern problem—for there is little comfort in that—but that Jesus knew something of what it meant and that He cared. If Christians had taken more seriously not only this story but the whole teaching of Jesus, there might still be periods of bad trade—though even that is not certain—but the whole character of the "unemployment problem" would have been transformed.

My old teacher, Sir Henry Jones, used to tell his classes that the most pathetic line in all Shakespeare was this: "Othello's occupation's gone." By his daily work man is not only providing food and shelter for himself and his family, he is also taking his place in the life of the community. The real tragedy of unemployment is not merely that it involves in all too many cases—in spite of insurance benefits—a lowering of an already too low standard of living; the real tragedy is the absence of occupation, and the heaviest burden upon the unemployed man—and the finer he is the heavier is the burden—is the sense that he is not wanted, that he is not taking his share in the common life. Nothing is more miserable than an "idle" man, and there are no more pitiable figures than the young men who have *never* had a job at all.

Perhaps one day we shall be able to arrange

affairs so that the productive capacity of the community will be employed to meet the needs of the community, and that the leisure made possible by that productive capacity shall be distributed among all as leisure and not as "unemployment." A more earnest attention to the teachings of Jesus would inspire us to seek for and find the technical methods of finance, economics, and industrial management by which this could be made possible. Industry was made for man; not man for industry: that surely is a deduction from the Gospels that would carry us a long way.

But it is not likely that Jesus spoke this parable directly with a view to its bearing upon agricultural hours and wages. He was thinking, rather, of the motives and the rewards of the service of God. An employer who habitually treated his workers on such a basis as is suggested here would soon have labor disputes on his hands, as the parable recognizes, and be forced out of business by his competitors. In the ancient world, as in the modern world, goods were distributed according to earnings, and earnings were decided by what a man could exact from his employer, not by his needs. But in the family the father gives in accordance with need, not with earning capacity. The way of the family is the way of the kingdom of God. Perhaps it is not "just," but then God does not deal with men on principles of abstract justice. He sends His rain upon the fields of the righteous and unrighteous alike, and His sun shines on the evil and the good. "In the course of justice none of us should see salvation." At least

God never gives men less than they deserve but always more.

Certainly, the man who sets out to serve Christ upon a basis of "nicely calculated less or more," or for the sake of reward here or hereafter, has not understood the spirit of his Master. Service never constitutes a claim of right against God or a corresponding reward at all. We must always remain in His debt.[7]

Christian service is service done for the love of it. A great American educationalist is reported to have thanked his Board for paying him to do his work. He declared he would gladly have paid them for the privilege of being allowed to do it if he had been wealthy enough. It is only in that spirit that a man can do a really good job in any realm of life. The Christian will pity from the bottom of his heart those who have joined his Master's service only at the eleventh hour and have missed the thrills and strains of a lifetime's labors. In a kingdom of love no one will stand on privilege.

Does this parable mean, then, that God rewards all His servants equally? Does John, the beloved disciple, enter heaven on the same level as the penitent thief? Is the martyr to get no more reward than the Christian whose religion has never disturbed his comfort? To ask the question is to show, as Peter's question showed, that we still miss the spirit of the Kingdom. Yet if there must be an answer, it surely is "No." The parables of the

---

[7] See further, "Unprofitable Servants," pp. 189ff.

pounds and the talents are in the teaching of Jesus
as well as this parable. There are degrees of
capacity for receiving the bounty of God. The
uneducated eye cannot appreciate the glories of the
Old Masters. The uneducated ear does not thrill
to the music of Bach. So the untrained soul on
entering the service of God is not on a level with
those whose lifelong endeavor has been to worship
Him and to do His will.

God does not treat all men alike, but He treats
all men in love. His verdicts are not arbitrary,
but they depend upon different tests from those
current among men.

Further, it must be remembered that the reward
of faithful service in the Kingdom is the opportunity for still greater service. The greatest there
is he who serves the most. And the true servant of
Christ will rejoice to have it so. The joy of the
Lord is to serve, and to enter into that joy is the
highest reward of faithful discipleship.

"So will I gather hope and strength anew,
  For I do know, God's patient love perceives
Not what we did, but what we tried to do;
And though the ripened ears be sadly few,
  He will accept our sheaves."

# XXIII

## THE TALENTS AND THE POUNDS

He went on to tell a parable in their hearing, as he was approaching Jerusalem and as they imagined God's Reign would instantly come into view. "A nobleman," he said, "went abroad to obtain royal power for himself and then return. He first called his ten servants, giving them each a five-pound note, and telling them, 'Trade with this till I come back.' Now his people hated him and sent envoys after him to say, 'We object to him having royal power over us.' However he secured the royal power and came home. Then he ordered the servants to be called who had been given the money, that he might find out what business they had done. The first came up saying, 'Your five pounds has made other fifty, sir.' 'Capital,' he said, 'you excellent servant! because you have proved trustworthy in a trifle, you are placed over ten towns.' Then the second came and said, 'Your five pounds has made twenty-five, sir.' To him he said, 'And you are set over five towns.' Then the next came and said, 'Here is your five pounds, sir; I kept it safe in a napkin, for I was afraid of you, you are such a hard man—picking up what you never put down, and reaping what you never sowed.' He replied, 'You rascal of a servant, I will convict you by what you have said yourself. You knew, did you, that I was a hard man, picking up what I never put down, and reaping what I never sowed! Why then did you not put my money into the bank, so that I could have got it with interest when I came back?' Then he said to the bystanders, 'Take the five pounds from him and gave it to the man with fifty.' 'Sir,' they said, 'he has fifty already!' 'I tell you,

'to everyone who has shall more be given,
    but from him who has nothing, even what he has
        shall be taken.

'And now for these enemies of mine who objected to
me reigning over them—bring them here and slay
them in my presence.' "—*Luke* 19. 11-27.

For the case is that of a man going abroad, who
summoned his servants and handed over his property
to them; to one he gave twelve hundred pounds, to
another five hundred, and to another two hundred and
fifty; each got according to his capacity. Then the
man went abroad. The servant who had got the
twelve hundred pounds at once went and traded with
them, making another twelve hundred. Similarly the
servant who had got the five hundred pounds made
another five hundred. But the servant who had got the
two hundred and fifty pounds went off and dug a hole
in the ground and hid his master's money. Now a
long time afterward the master of those servants came
back and settled accounts with them. Then the servant who had got the twelve hundred pounds came
forward, bringing twelve hundred more; he said, "You
handed me twelve hundred pounds, sir; here I have
gained another twelve hundred." His master said to
him, "Capital, you excellent and trusty servant! You
have been trusty in charge of a small sum: I will put
you in charge of a large sum. Come and share your
master's feast." Then the servant with the five hundred pounds came forward. He said, "You handed me
five hundred pounds, sir; here I have gained another
five hundred." His master said to him, "Capital, you
excellent and trusty servant! You have been trusty in
charge of a small sum: I will put you in charge of a
large sum. Come and share your master's feast."
Then the servant who had got the two hundred and
fifty pounds came forward. He said, "I knew you were
a hard man, sir, reaping where you never sowed and
gathering where you never winnowed. So I was
afraid; I went and hid your two hundred and fifty

pounds in the earth.  There's your money!"  His master said to him in reply, "You rascal, you idle servant!  You knew, did you, that I reap where I have
never sowed and gather where I have never winnowed?
Well then, you should have handed my money to the
bankers and I would have got my capital with interest when I came back.  Take therefore the two hundred and fifty pounds away from him, give it to the
servant who had the twelve hundred.

"For to everyone who has shall more be given and
richly given;
but from him who has nothing, even what he has
shall be taken.

"Throw the good-for-nothing servant into the darkness
outside; there men will wail and gnash their teeth."
—*Matthew* 25. 14-30.

THE exact relationship between these two
parables is not easy to determine, and scholars
and commentators are very divided in their views.
Clearly, there are both similarities and differences.
The main theme, of faithfulness in the use of opportunity, is the same, but the setting is different.
Some scholars hold that both come from a single
original, and that Matthew's version is more likely
to be correct.  A careful reading of Luke's story
certainly might suggest that two different stories
have been combined.  There is the story of a king
who goes to Rome to receive confirmation of his
rule from the emperor, and who deals severely on
his return with those subjects who had opposed his
election[1] (verses 11-12, 14, 15a, 27).  Side by side

---

[1] The parable of the pounds was told at Jericho, and no doubt
speaker and hearers alike would think of Archelaus.  The
elder of the two sons of Herod the Great, he had Judea bequeathed to him.  He went to Rome to receive confirmation of

with it is the detachable story of his testing ten of his servants as to their ability for higher rank in his kingdom by giving them each a pound to trade with —a story very similar to that which Matthew tells, and even with verbal identities (verses 11-13, 15-26).

On the other hand, there are clear differences between the two parables, even when the rebellion in Luke's story is removed. In the parable of the talents the original endowments are different in amount, and the servants are commended in the same terms for having achieved proportionate returns on their capital. In the parable of the pounds the initial gift is equal and the promotion awarded is in strict proportion to the size of the increase achieved—ten cities for ten pounds, five cities for five pounds. It is difficult to believe that these changes are due to faulty transmission or to deliberate editing. It seems far more likely that there are two distinct parables using the same fundamental theme and enforcing the same main lesson. There is, of course, no reason why our Lord should not have used the same theme with different audiences and have used it with variations to suit the occasion as every speaker does. We create unnecessary difficulties for ourselves if we assume gratuitously that He can never have "repeated Himself."

The fundamental theme is the necessity for faithfulness in the use of opportunities. The following comments are chiefly based upon the parable of the talents as the more detailed of the two.

---

the bequest from Augustus. A deputation of eighty of his subjects presented a counter petition, alleging misgovernment. Caesar, however, gave him the kingdom, though with the title of ethnarch instead of king.

We have got so used to the word "talent" as meaning natural endowment of any kind that we often forget that it entered the language from this parable. Its modern use in the wider sense is a legitimate interpretation of the parable, but originally, of course, the talent was a sum of money. It is difficult, with the incessant variation of monetary values and purchasing power in the intervening centuries, to fix an exact equivalent in modern English money. Commentators vary very widely. It was, however, a large sum. A quite modest estimate makes one talent equal $1,200 (the pound might represent more in modern currency, or "a five pound note," as Moffatt renders it).

The servants were given talents in accordance with their abilities; to one five, to another two, to another one. The master did not want to overburden the weak or underemploy the able. The varying distribution was not arbitrary. Is this meant as a recognition of the patent but often ignored fact that men are *not* equal? Men may be equal in worth to God. They may be, as the parable emphasizes, equal in faithful effort. But equal in capacity and ability they certainly are not. There is much to be said in favor of democracy on Christian grounds, but it would do none of us any harm to consider carefully in what sense, if any, men can truly be said to be "equal."

The emphasis falls upon the man with one talent, and the use he makes of his endowment. How true to life he is! The one-talented man is always tempted to mistrust himself. He suffers, as we say nowadays, from "an inferiority complex." It may lead to bluster and the production of all sorts of reasons—"rationalizations"—as to why he has not achieved great results. It certainly is not *his* fault. Circumstances have been too much for him. People have been unjust; his master is "hard" and expects impossibilities. The truth is, he feels that he is not able to achieve anything very great, and so he will not try to do anything at all. He is timid and lacking in self-confidence. He secretly envies the abilities of others. And only too often he has to suffer the impatience of the strong and the clever at his weakness.

It is often a rude awakening when we discover our limitations and realize we must be content with less than the rosy dreams of youth had promised. Most of us, after all, are just ordinary folk, and we shall not achieve happiness and effectiveness in life until we admit it. Some people are soured when the facts can no longer be denied. They can never be happy on the back benches. They picture themselves as addressing Congress from a front-row seat, if only life had not been so unjust.

Abraham Lincoln said that "God must love the common people, because He has made so many of us." We need the genius and the leader, but we need the ordinary man too, to do the daily work of the world. The great statesman cannot lead his nation forward without the sympathy and support of the common people. The man of five talents could achieve little without the rest of us with our two talents and our one.

God wants the service of the men of great ability, but when He comes to balance the books many who were first shall be last, and the last first. He does not judge by success but by effort, not by achievement but by faithfulness. We shall not be blamed for having only two talents or one. We shall be judged in accordance with our use of what we have got. Jesus said that the poor widow who cast her farthing into the treasury put in more than all the others. God's judgment of the true worth of men is based upon different standards from those of society.

The man who did not use his talent lost it. That was no arbitrary decision. It is a law of life. Physically, mentally, morally, spiritually, we lose the powers we do not use; those we use grow in the using. "In the moral world," wrote Edward Caird, "standing still is going back." The one talent might have become two had it been faithfully used. To him that uses shall be given. Faithfulness is all. The overcautiousness in the use of the talent was really a breach of trust. For the talent was not his; it was only lent him for use.

Is the concluding verse (30) really part of the parable? If the "outer darkness" is a reference to Gehenna—and the phraseology is familiar in Jewish eschatological writing—it is impossible to understand why the lord in the parable should claim the power or the right to consign his servant to hell. We have no justification for identifying the master with God. The verse must be "in character" with the lord of the parable. As Oesterley remarks: "The servant has already been punished by being deprived of the talent; a second punishment, especially one of this nature, is not called for; nor is this punishment commensurate with the offense; the talent was brought back, it was not stolen."[2]   He accordingly holds that the verse is a later addition, intended to give the parable an eschatological moral which does not in reality belong to it.

Another interpretation favored by some commentators makes the verse refer merely to the black night outside the master's house.   That explanation would fit well with the wedding feast which took place at night, and with the exclusion of the unworthy guest from the banqueting hall (Matthew 22. 13).   But it does not fit the scene of this parable.

Luke, by his introductory verse, clearly intends the parable to make clear that Jesus foretold a delay before His return.   It was told, he says, because they supposed the kingdom of God would immediately appear.   In fact, the king is going a long journey first.   This point is more fully discussed in the Introduction.[3]

Dodd suggests, very acutely, that by the man with the one talent our Lord may mean the pious Jews who sought only to preserve the religion and the law intact and uncontaminated.   The message given them by God to be passed on to the world they hoarded.   They rejected their missionary vocation.   It was not till the early Church took the torch from their faltering hands and "turned to the Gentiles" that the light began to shine as it was intended.   It is risky to invest capital, but without running that risk you will gain no interest.

[2] *Op. cit.*, p. 149.
[3] Page 34ff.

# XXIV

## THE TWO SONS

A man had two sons. He went to the first and said, "Son, go and work in the vineyard today;" he replied, "I will go, sir," but he did not go. The man went to the second and said the same to him; he replied, "I will not," but afterward he changed his mind and did go. Which of the two did the will of the father? They said, "The last." Jesus said to them, "I tell you truly, the taxgatherers and harlots are going into the Realm of God before you. For John showed you the way to be good and you would not believe him; the taxgatherers and harlots believed him, and even though you saw that, you would not change your mind afterward and believe him."—*Matthew* 21. 28-32.

MATTHEW clearly implies, by his setting of them, that the parables of the two sons, the wicked husbandmen, and the wedding feast were all prompted by the events described in verses 1-27 of this twenty-seventh chapter. The anger of the priests and scribes had been roused by the triumphal entry, the cleansing of the Temple, and by the nature of His teaching in the Temple precincts. As the religious authorities they obviously could not ignore His doings, and particularly the deliberate claim to be the Messiah involved in His mode of entry to the city (see Zechariah 9. 9) and by implication in the cleansing of the Temple. So they ask for His credentials. "By what authority doest thou these things?" (Verse 23.)

But our Lord suggests that they have proved
themselves incompetent as judges of spiritual
authority by their inability to pronounce on the
claims of John the Baptist. He goes on to tell
the story of the Two Sons.

Like the parable of the prodigal son, this tells
of the two sons of a farmer and their relation to
their father. There is some doubt in the manuscripts as to which of the two sons comes first in
the story, and the Authorized Version follows a
different story from the Revised. But the tenor
of the story is quite clear. Here we follow the
order of the Revised and of Moffatt.

The father asked his two sons to go and work
in the vineyard. The first replied at once in
respectful tones, "Yes, sir, I will." But he never
went. The second son replied, rudely, "No, I
won't." But on second thought he was sorry for
his refusal and went. "Which of these boys,"
asked Jesus of His hearers, apparently the chief
priests and elders in the Temple, "did his father's
will, the one who spoke politely and did nothing,
or the one who in spite of his rude behavior
actually went to the vineyard?" "The second one,
of course," they replied, doubtless surprised at
being asked so obvious a question. "Can't you
see," went on Jesus, "that you are condemning
yourselves? You profess great eagerness for obedience to the will of God, and you can talk most
impressively on religious topics. But although you
cannot deny that John the Baptist has come with
a divine message you refuse to do anything about
it. Yet the publicans and harlots who openly

scoffed at religion have listened to him and
repented of their evil past. They are actually
showing you the way into the kingdom of God."

Both sons, of course, were in the wrong. The
son who went was wrong to speak so to his
father. The polite son was wrong in breaking his
promise. But one repented of his faults: the other
did not.

The two sons are still with us—those who make
great religious professions but whose lives do not
correspond, and the professedly irreligious whose
lives are sometimes better than their creed.

Many of us let talk about religion take the
place of religious living. It is terribly easy to let
religiosity become a substitute for real religion,
to lull oneself to a dreadful complacency by
attendance at church and all kinds of pious per-
formances, and yet in spite of it all to lack the
real thing. The son probably intended to go. He
knew that he ought to work in the vineyard, and
he would not for the world be rude to his father.
His answer was all that could be desired, but *he
did not go*.

One might almost dare to say that there is
danger in our very familiarity with the teachings
and claims of Jesus. We get used to His words
and they no longer startle and search us. We
assent to them cordially but they do not provoke
us into taking them seriously. There is no one
of us who can read the Beatitudes, for example,
slowly and thoughtfully, with an honest attempt to
apply them to his own life without being painfully
aware of how far short his life comes of his Chris-

tian profession. It is by no means obvious what the Christian life involves in the modern world, but so many of us are not trying to find out. We are content to sing hymns about it. Are you not sometimes stabbed to the heart by some great hymn as you suddenly realize what the familiar words mean? "I have no right to be singing this," you think. Happy are we, then, if we do not let our resolve for a more serious discipleship fade away with the Benediction.

"Not every one that saith unto me, Lord, Lord, shall enter into the kingdom of God, but he that doeth the will of my Father which is in heaven."

No doubt there are real hypocrites still in the churches today, people who, just for the sake of profit or men's approval, pretend a goodness they do not possess and do not desire. But it may be suspected that there is almost more hypocrisy in the other camp today. There is not much worldly advantage in going to church, and in some quarters it takes a good deal of moral courage to be known as a Christian. So there are hypocrites today who pretend to a cynicism or even a wickedness that they do not possess. They like to be thought "men of the world," and in language and attitude they do violence to ideals that they secretly respect.

Curiously enough, these are the people who think that hypocrisy is the crowning sin. "I make no pretense to be a saint," they tell you, and almost expect to be applauded because they do not aspire to goodness. The real hypocrite is certainly a repellent person, but is it really any more pleasant to pretend to be worse than you are because you have not enough strength of mind to stand up for your convictions? If we feel we ought to do the will of God, if we really believe that decency and unselfishness matter, let us say so.

It is a horrible thing to profess to follow Christ and to deny Him in life. But it is no less horrible a thing to deny Him in word as well as in life. "But surely Jesus in the parable praised those who said, 'No'?" Never! He praised those who repented of saying "No," and went and did their father's will.

What are we *doing* about it?

# XXV

## THE WICKED HUSBANDMEN

Listen to another parable.  There was a householder who *planted a vineyard, put a fence round it, dug a wine-vat inside it, and built a watchtower:* then he leased it to vinedressers and went abroad.  When the fruit-season was near, he sent his servants to the vine-dressers to collect his fruit; but the vinedressers took his servants and flogged one, killed another, and stoned a third.  Once more he sent some other servants, more than he had sent at first, and they did the same to them.  Afterward he sent them his son; "They will respect my son," he said.  But when the vinedressers saw his son they said to themselves, "Here is the heir; come on, let us kill him and seize his inheritance!" So they took and threw him outside the vineyard and killed him.  Now, when the owner of the vineyard comes, what will he do to these vinedressers?  They replied, "He will utterly destroy the wretches and lease the vineyard to other vinedressers who will give him the fruits in their season."  Jesus said to them, "Have you never read in the scriptures,

*"The stone that the builders rejected*
*is the chief stone now of the corner:*
*this is the doing of the Lord,*
*and a wonder to our eyes?*

"I tell you therefore that the Realm of God will be taken from you and given to a nation that bears the fruits of the Realm.

["Everyone who falls on this stone will be shattered, and whoever it falls upon will be crushed."]

220

When the high priests and Pharisees heard these parables they knew he was speaking about them; they tried to get hold of him, but they were afraid of the crowds, as the crowds held him to be a prophet.— *Matthew* 21. 33-46.

Then he proceeded to address them in parables. "A man *planted a vineyard, fenced it round, dug a trough for the winepress, and built a tower;* then he leased it to vinedressers and went abroad. When the season came round he sent a servant to the vinedressers to collect from the vinedressers some of the produce of the vineyard, but they took and flogged him and sent him off with nothing. Once more he sent them another servant; him they knocked on the head and insulted. He sent another, but they killed him. And so they treated many others; some they flogged and some they killed. He had still one left, a beloved son; he sent him to them last, saying, 'They will respect my son.' But these vinedressers said to themselves, 'Here is the heir; come on, let us kill him, and the inheritance will be our own.' So they took and killed him, and threw him outside the vineyard. Now what will the owner of the vineyard do? He will come and destroy the vinedressers, and he will give the vineyard to others. Have you not even read this scripture?—

*"The stone that the builders rejected is the chief*
*stone now of the corner:*
*this is the doing of the Lord,*
*and a wonder to our eyes."*

Then they tried to get hold of him, but they were afraid of the multitude. They knew he had meant the parable for them.—*Mark* 12. 1-12.

Then he proceeded to tell the people the following parable. "A man *planted a vineyard,* leased it to vinedressers, and went abroad for some time. When the season came round he sent a servant to the vinedressers to receive part of the produce of the vineyard, but the vinedressers flogged him and sent him off with nothing.  He proceeded to send another servant, and they flogged him too, insulted him and sent him off with nothing.  Then he sent still a third, but this one they wounded and threw outside.  Said the owner of the vineyard, 'What shall I do?  I will send my beloved son; perhaps they will respect him.'  But when the vinedressers saw him, they argued to themselves, 'Here is the heir, let us kill him, so that the inheritance may be ours.'  And they threw him outside the vineyard and killed him.  Now what will the owner of the vineyard do to them?  He will come and kill these vinedressers and give the vineyard to others."  When they heard that, they said, "God forbid!"  But he looked at them and said, "Then what does this scripture mean?—

> *"The stone that the builders rejected is the chief stone now of the corner.*
> Everyone who falls on that stone will be shattered, and whoever it falls upon will be crushed."

At that hour the scribes and high priests tried to lay hands on him, but they were afraid of the people.  They knew he had meant this parable for them.—*Luke* 20. 9-19.

WRITERS on this parable have often commented on the outrageous and impossible conduct of the husbandmen.  The story, they urge, does not ring true of ordinary life; it is an allegory of the relations of God with the human race.  But it is not safe to argue from conditions in modern England or America.  In Palestine, and especially in Galilee, in the time of Christ there was considerable political unrest.  Large estates were often held by foreigners, and agrarian discontent might go hand in hand with nationalist feeling, as it did in pre-war Ireland.  So it is not unthinkable that the refusal of rent might be the prelude to murder and the forcible seizure of land by the peasantry. "The parable, in fact, so far from being an artificially constructed allegory, may be taken as evidence of the kind of thing that went on in Galilee during the half-century preceding the general revolt of 66 A. D."[1]

Nevertheless, the parable is more allegorical in character than most of the others. The vineyard was a recognized prophetic symbol for the Jewish nation. Jesus' hearers could not help thinking, as He told His tale, of such familiar passages as Isaiah 5. 1-7; Psalm 80. 8-16; Isaiah 27. 1-6; Jeremiah 2. 21; and others might be cited. It was an old theme with a new application. The trend of the story got clearer and clearer, till the audience[2] was stung into protest.

The authenticity of the parable has been questioned, because of its explicit claim of Messiahship and because the death of Jesus is assumed. But the claims of Jesus did become more clearly formulated and more public as His ministry proceeded, as much else in the Gospels shows. It may be conceded that the change made by Matthew (21. 39) and Luke (20. 15) in Mark's account of the place of the Son's death (Mark 12. 8) suggests a touching-up of the story after the event. But a parable which has been invented as a whole after the death of Jesus would have naturally contained some explicit reference to the resurrection.

After the succession of servants sent to collect

---

[1] Dodd, *The Parables of the Kingdom*, p. 125.
[2] See the introductory paragraphs to the chapter on "The Two Sons," p. 215.

the rent of the vineyard—probably in kind—and
meeting with ill treatment, and even death, the
owner sends his son.[3]   This is an unmistakable
assertion of the claim of our Lord to hold a different status from the prophets who went before Him.
We need not read into it a claim to divinity,
though, of course, it is consistent with that.   But
it is at least a definite claim to be the Messiah,
the one in whom the purposes of God were to
be embodied and worked out.   He comes at the
crisis of Israel's history.   He is God's last appeal.
His rejection, now determined upon by the leaders
of the nation, would lead not only to suffering
for the nation but to its disinheritance.   Another
community, the true Israel, the Church of the
Christ, would inherit the Kingdom.

The parable throws impressive light upon the
self-consciousness of Jesus, and the implied claim
is all the more striking because it comes almost
incidentally in the course of the story.   The quotation that follows the parable is from the 118th
Psalm, regarded by the rabbis as applying to the
Messiah, and is therefore in itself a further assertion of His claim.   It is also a stern warning to His
audience that they will not have got rid of Him
by killing Him.[4]

[3] Stephen in his speech to his murderers might almost be
commenting on the parable.   Acts 7. 51-53.

[4] Oesterley, however, holds that the quotation from Psalm 118
has no real point of contact with the parable, and that the text
reads better without it.   The quotation means that the son, that
is, the rejected stone, who has been put to death is to be restored
gloriously.   This does not fit the content and purpose of the
parable.   "There is much, therefore, to be said for the con-
tention that this quotation was inserted later by a Christian
believer."   Op. cit., p. 121.

The claims made by Jesus for Himself must be reckoned with in any estimate of His personality. The Synoptic Gospels contain by implication, and almost in so many words, claims as startling and far-reaching as any made on His behalf in the fourth Gospel or the writings of the apostle Paul. They cannot all be explained away as later interpolations. (See, for example, the Synoptic stories of the Baptism, the Temptation, the Transfiguration. Matthew 11. 28-30; Luke 19. 23-26; 10. 22, etc.)

Amazing also is the calm challenge of the parable to his enemies. It is told by all three evangelists near the end of the ministry when the Jewish leaders had taken their decision. "Do you realize where your attitude is leading you? You are plotting my murder." It is plain speaking indeed, and His audience knew perfectly well what He was saying. When Jesus told them that the inevitable outcome would be the loss by the nation of its place of honor and privilege in the divine purpose, the hearers exclaimed, "God forbid!" And Jesus "looked upon them." The way Jesus had of looking at people is often mentioned in the Gospels as characteristic of Him—a searching, steady gaze of love, or sorrow, or judgment, or anger—an unforgettable look. So now, Jesus looked at them and quoted the stern words of the psalm, "What then is this that is written,

"The stone which the builders rejected
The same was made the head of the corner?

". . . And the scribes and the chief priests sought

to lay hands on him in that very hour, . . . for they perceiveth that he spake this parable against them" (Luke 20. 17-19).

This parable illustrates one of the values in the parabolic method of teaching referred to in the Introduction.[5] A direct challenge in so many words to His hearers would probably not have been listened to. But the impersonal approach made the audience judge itself. The familiar theme would catch their attention and they would wonder what the application was to be. Not till the parable developed could they realize that its point was directed against them. One may compare the skill with which Nathan awakened David's sympathy for the victim of an oppressor, and made him commit himself to restitution before the dramatic disclosure, "Thou art the man!" (2 Samuel 12. 1-14).

Did, then, the Jewish leaders know what they were doing? Doubtless they would have denied strenuously that Jesus was "the Son," the Messiah. That they already intended to put Him out of the way if He persisted in His propaganda they would probably have admitted. But they had their justification: "It is expedient for us that one man should die for the people, and that the whole nation perish not" (John 11. 47-53). Doubtless many of them were sincere in believing that what they did they did for the good of the nation. Perhaps some of them were included in the prayer, "Father, forgive them, for they know not what they do."

---

[5] Page 18.

We can see as clearly as the bystanders the application to the leaders of Israel. Has the parable perhaps an application to the Christian Church of today? There are vested interests in all the churches. We may sometimes be in danger of thinking that the Church exists for its own sake, or, worse still, for the sake of those of us who in some measure control its affairs. And we may be resentful at demands for the payment of rent to the real Owner. Not that we should refuse God if He came in person! But then He usually collects His dues incognito—as an Indian outcaste, a worker in the African copper belt, an unemployed man at home, a demand for sacrifice in support of some task of evangelism or of social betterment. Sometimes they may seem to cut across the interests of the Church as an ecclesiastical institution, by reducing its income, perhaps, or by bringing it into conflict with political authority. . . . We need to beware lest in defense of the Vineyard we reject the orders of its Lord.

# XXVI

## THE TEN VIRGINS

Then shall the Realm of heaven be compared to ten maidens who took their lamps and went out to meet the bridegroom and the bride.[1] Five of them were stupid and five were sensible. For although the stupid took their lamps, they took no oil with them, whereas the sensible took oil in their vessels as well as their lamps. As the bridegroom was long of coming, they all grew drowsy and went to sleep. But at midnight the cry arose, "Here is the bridegroom! Come out to meet him!" Then all the maidens rose and trimmed their lamps. The stupid said to the sensible, "Give us some of your oil, for our lamps are going out." But the sensible replied, "No, there may not be enough for us and for you. Better go to the dealers and buy for yourselves." Now while they were away buying oil, the bridegroom arrived; those maidens who were ready accompanied him to the marriage-banquet, and the door was shut. Afterward the rest of the maidens came and said, "Oh sir, oh sir, open the door for us!" but he replied, "I tell you frankly, I do not know you." Keep on the watch then, for you know neither the day nor the hour.—*Matthew* 25. 1-13.

THIS is a difficult parable. On the surface it seems simple enough, and the dramatic quality of it has captured men's imaginations and inspired many pictures and poems, but when one tries to

---

[1] The words καὶ τῆς νύμφης are added by D X*, the Latin and Syriac versions, etc. Their omission may have been due to the feeling of the later Church that Jesus as the Bridegroom ought alone to be mentioned.

probe for the inner meaning of it all, it is surprisingly elusive.   The expositors have been as baffled
as the poets and painters have been fascinated.   The
story itself is difficult to follow in detail, and it is
hard to be sure what lesson it is intended to convey.
The allegorizers have laid their hands upon it and
destroyed the dramatic vigor of the story without
making it yield its secret.   They can tell you why
there are ten bridesmaids, why the wise were exactly as many as the foolish, what the lamp and the
oil represent, what the sleep symbolizes, and much
more; but it is all dreadfully uninspiring.   Their
symbolisms are completely arbitrary, and each com-
mentator   dismisses   as   impossible   the   ingenious
scheme of his predecessors.   If it is not quite as
bad as that, it seems so, and even Calvin, who could
indulge at times in a good deal of allegorizing himself, is roused to protest by the treatment of this
parable.

The setting of the Eastern marriage is strange to
our Western experience, and much that was of
everyday familiarity to our Lord's hearers is therefore puzzling to us.   Unhappily, the key seems to
have been lost.   To consult book after book about
Eastern wedding customs is to find much difference
of opinion.   No doubt customs varied from country to country, and even perhaps from town to
town.   It is not easy to be sure just what the bridesmaids were doing.   It is better to admit ignorance,
especially as the meaning of the parable does not
seem to be greatly affected.   This much seems clear:
Ten bridesmaids are to meet the bridegroom and
escort him to the home of the bride, or, perhaps, to

share in the formal bringing home of the bride to her future home.  The wedding is at night and the bridesmaids equip themselves with torches to carry in the procession.  Probably the torches (not "lamps" as the Authorized Version says) were dishes containing a cloth wick dipped in oil, carried on top of a short wooden stem.  There is an unexpected and unexplained delay in the arrival of the bridegroom.  The bridesmaids all fall asleep. Suddenly at midnight they are awakened by the news of his coming.  Five of the bridesmaids find that their torches are going out.  They beg for oil from the others, but these have none to spare and advise them to try to buy some.  This they do, but when they return, the bridegroom has come.  The door is shut and they are refused admission.

One of the difficulties of the story is the harsh answer of the bridegroom to the late arrivals.  It does not seem in keeping with the situation.  The fact that the house is presumably not his but the home of the bride's father adds to the puzzle— though some scholars hold that the party has now returned to the bridegroom's house.  Our Lord might, of course, deliberately make him act in a way that no ordinary bridegroom would act, but one cannot help suspecting that the story has been amended.  It has been pointed out that "the last clause of verse 10 and verses 11 and 12 are largely the same as part of the metaphorical description of Judgment in Luke 13. 25-27, where they fit their context much better."[2]

What is the lesson our Lord intended to teach

---

[2] Cadoux, *The Parables of Jesus*, p. 70.

by the parable? Many expositors have assumed
that the "bridegroom" represents Christ Himself,
and that the story relates to "the Second Coming."
But this is by no means certain. One of our Lord's
constant themes was alertness, readiness for the
call of duty. It is straining the words to make them
always refer to an event still in the future after
two thousand years.[3]

We can at any rate with some confidence declare
that the necessity for spiritual preparedness is the
theme of the parable, whatever its immediate
application. The point must lie in the difference
between the wise and the foolish virgins. They
all slept—so the lesson cannot lie there. But the
wise went to sleep equipped and ready; the foolish
did not. There was no lack of goodwill in the
foolish bridesmaids. They were just as anxious
as the others to share in the festivities. But they
were thoughtless. Their lack of readiness was
not due to deliberate neglect, but to lack of foresight. Because of their stupidity, when the long-
looked-for moment arrived they missed their
opportunity. "They that were ready went in to
the marriage feast"—that is the keynote.

Jesus often says in varying metaphor, "Why cannot men bring to the service of God and His Kingdom that intelligence and forethought which is
expected of them in the ordinary affairs of life?"[4]

The event was sudden. If preparations had not

---

[3] It is impossible here to embark upon a discussion of the
vexed question of the real teaching of Jesus about the Second
Coming. The present writer has given his own views at length
in his book, *The Necessity of the Second Coming.*

[4] See on the parable of the unjust steward, p. 174.

been made before, it was too late to make them now. The emergency revealed with startling clearness the real character of the actors.

The reply of the wise virgins to the foolish ones strikes us perhaps as unkind.  But on reflection it appears more reasonable.  If the result of lending the oil was to be that all ten would probably be unable to play their proper part in the procession, there would have been no gain to anybody.  And if the story be applied, as it is meant to be, to the realm of character, the reply is inevitable: "There are things that can neither be lent nor borrowed."[5]  You cannot borrow another's Christian character; you must grow your own.  You cannot improvise a strong will.  It is true in the physical realm.  If a misused and unhealthy body has to meet a sudden assault of disease, it may be too late then to set to work to create a sound constitution. The penalty for past thoughtlessness may be fatal, however eager friends and doctors may be to help. A serene faith in immortality cannot be suddenly acquired when death visits your home.  It has its roots in an established and tested faith in the love of God.

The sudden midnight cry reveals the personality that the past years have been building.

[5] Shafto, *The Stories of the Kingdom*, p. 149.

# XXVII

## THE SHEEP AND THE GOATS

When the Son of man comes in his glory and *all the angels with him,* then he will sit on the throne of his glory, and all nations will be gathered in front of him; he will separate them one from another, as a shepherd separates the sheep from the goats, setting the sheep on his right hand and the goats on his left. Then shall the King say to those on his right, "Come, you whom my Father has blessed, come into your inheritance in the realm prepared for you from the foundation of the world.

"For I was hungry and you fed me,
  I was thirsty and you gave me drink,
I was a stranger and you entertained me,
  I was unclothed and you clothed me,
I was ill and you looked after me,
  I was in prison and you visited me."

Then the just will answer,

"Lord, when did we see you hungry and fed you? or
  thirsty and gave you drink?
when did we see you a stranger and entertain you?
  or unclothed and clothed you?
when did we see you ill or in prison and visit you?"

The King will answer them, "I tell you truly, in so far as you did it to one of these brothers of mine, even to the least of them, you did it to me." Then he will say to those on the left, "Begone from me, you accursed ones, to the eternal fire which has been prepared for the devil and his angels!

"For I was hungry but you never fed me,
    I was thirsty but you never gave me drink,
I was a stranger but you never entertained me,
    I was unclothed but you never clothed me,
I was ill and in prison but you never looked after
    me."

Then they will answer too, "Lord, when did we ever see you hungry or thirsty or a stranger or unclothed or ill or in prison, and did not minister to you?" Then he will answer them, "I tell you truly, in so far as you did not do it to one of these, even the least of them, you did not do it to me."

So they shall depart to eternal punishment,
    and the just to eternal life.—*Matthew* 25. 31-46.

THIS is omitted altogether from many books on the parables, but the reasons for ruling it out seem somewhat arbitrary. One recent writer, for example, says that the only parabolic element is the simile of the shepherd separating the sheep and the goats, and that this is only a passing allusion. Yet surely it may be a parable even if it is not about sheep and goats. The picture of a royal throne before which the nations are gathered for judgment is a metaphorical picture of spiritual reality in terms of human life, and so a parable.

## I. THE FACT OF JUDGMENT

In our time there has been a blurring of the lines of moral distinction. The moral standards of our grandfathers have collapsed. Many doubt if, indeed, there are such things at all. Mr. J. W. N. Sullivan, discussing this modern attitude, says:

"Sins have been more or less turned into amiable weaknesses, but also sanctity and heroism have become myths. The human being as a whole has been made smaller. The novelists have convinced us that the average human being is compounded out of a few paltry vices and a fairly large slab of good nature. Christ, who called us sons of God, and Swift, who called us odious little vermin, are both making a quite unnecessary fuss about almost nothing."[1]

Jesus is in no doubt that men will be judged. The parables alone insist upon it many times. Make as much allowance for metaphor as you wish—there is a Judgment. Conduct matters. Good is good and bad is bad. As Bishop Butler lay dying he said, "It is an awful thing to appear before the moral Governor of the world."

Some have protested that it is impossible to put people neatly into two categories like this. Some men's characters no doubt are clearly black or clearly white—like Syrian goats and sheep. But surely most of us are gray.

Jesus holds that fundamentally there is a distinction. Men are on one side or the other—for God and goodness or against Him. They vary infinitely among themselves in the distance they have got along the road to personal goodness. But it is the direction in which they are facing that matters. "God deals with us," said Saint Augustine, "not as we are but as we are becoming." The Judge knows. He can tell as unerringly as the

---

[1] *But For the Grace of God*, pp. 117-18.

shepherd's eye can pick out the sheep in his flock
from the goats.

Men may live uncertainly for a time, but no
ultimate neutrality is possible. The essential man
is on one side or the other. "He that is not for
me is against me." Some build on rock, some on
sand. There are tares among the wheat. There
is a broad way and a narrow way.

## II. THE JUDGE

Who is he? Jesus, the speaker, the carpenter
from Nazareth. That is worth pondering. The
Galilean teacher, Himself within a few days of
judgment and sentence of death from the Church
and State, claims to be the ultimate Judge of "all
nations." Even if you eliminate this parable—and
there is no reason why you should—there are many
other such startling claims in the Gospels. They
must be faced by those who would have us regard Jesus as merely a great religious teacher. If
these seemingly extravagant claims are not true,
surely they destroy the greatness and reliability of
the teaching. If they are true, who can this man
be? The old dilemma is not forced. *"Aut Deus,
aut homo non bonus."* He is either God or He is
not a good man.

Scholars are agreed that the King in the parable
is the Messiah, and that Jesus claimed to be the
Messiah. Some, however, hold that the Son of
man in verse 31 is not the same as the King in
verse 34.[2] I cannot myself see the force of their

---

[2] So Manson, *Teaching of Jesus,* pp. 265ff.

arguments. The Son of man is seated on a throne and gathers the nations before Him and separates them. Then the King speaks. Surely the natural conclusion is that it is the same figure who was occupying the throne all the time.

This does not, of course, dispose of the many tangled problems regarding the meaning of the phrase, "the Son of man." I do not propose to attempt to discuss them here. There is no doubt that "the son of man" is used in Old Testament and apocalyptic writings as equivalent, not to an individual, but to the faithful Remnant or the Messianic kingdom or community. Some scholars hold that the phrase means this in the Gospels also. For my own part I agree with those who believe that Jesus used the term as a personal title and as an alternative for Messiah. Manson holds the former view, but believes that at the end of His life Jesus "is the Son of man because He alone is equal to the claims of the Son-of-man ideal. Son of man and Messiah have been united in one person, his person."[3] Nevertheless, he thinks that even in this parable the Son of man represents the "Kingdom of the Saints," of which Jesus is the Head.

## III. The Judged

The Greek words for "all nations" are usually employed for the non-Jewish peoples, the Gentiles. Many commentators believe that this parable represents the judgment of non-Christians who are

[3] *Op. cit.*, p. 268.

judged by the standard of love in action, an unconscious and not a conscious discipleship. But the whole context suggests the judgment of the whole human race, and the usage of the words does not forbid that.

## IV. THE STANDARD OF JUDGMENT

Love, in the teaching of Jesus, is the essence of true religion and the ultimate test of character. Those who love show their Father's likeness and are recognizable as His. The apostle was only echoing the thought of his Master when he wrote: "Though I speak with the tongues of men and of angels . . . though I have the gift of prophecy, and understand all mysteries and all knowledge; and though I have all faith, so that I could remove mountains . . . and though I bestow all my goods to feed the poor, and though I give my body to be burned, and have not charity, it profiteth me nothing" (1 Corinthians 13. 1-3).

Jesus' identification of Himself with the "under-dog" has inspired innumerable acts of devotion and sacrifice. One thinks of the Moravians, who in their missionary work deliberately choose to care for the "unimportant" people; of leper colonies; of care for the Indian outcaste; of the raising of the African from his savagery. One is reminded of John Howard, of whom Burke said that he had "visited all Europe—not to survey the sumptuousness of palaces or the stateliness of temples; not to make accurate measurements of the remains of ancient grandeur, nor to form a scale of the curiosity of modern art; not to collect

medals or collate manuscripts—but to dive into
the depths of dungeons and plunge into the in-
fection of hospitals; to survey the mansions of
sorrow and pain; to take the gauge and measure
of misery, depression, and contempt; to remember
the forgotten, to attend to the neglected, to visit
the forsaken, and compare and collate the miseries
of all men in all countries." And Howard is only
one of a great host in many centuries, famous and
unknown, who have found in the life of Jesus an
inspiration to the self-sacrificing service of the poor
and wretched.

Some commentators are troubled at the absence
of any credal requirements or theological standards
in this trial. They are anxious to remind us that
no parable can contain all the truth. Certainly,
there are all kinds of theological presuppositions
and implications to which our Lord does not here
refer. Yet, ought we to minimize the directness
of His words even if they are upsetting to some
of our susceptibilities? Without for a moment
depreciating the importance of a sound theology
we can never afford to forget the emphasis laid
by Jesus and by the New Testament generally upon
the central importance of love. By their fruits
men will know those who are His. It is a stern
test—but if we are not such people as He here
commends, will our irreproachable theology avail?
If we love not our brother whom we have seen,
how can we love God whom we have not seen?

### V. THE SENTENCE

The verdict was received with surprise by both

the condemned and the commended. Neither
had appreciated the significance of their actions.
Is it not characteristic of the finest spirits that
they seem completely unaware of the beauty and
devotion of their lives?

There seems to be a suggestion of snobbery
in the attitude of the condemned. "Of course,
Lord, if we had imagined for a moment that you
were interested in what became of people like
that, it would have been a pleasure to have looked
after them. But, really, we hardly thought it was
necessary to bother about *them*."

The judgment upon the condemned raises acute
problems which we cannot avoid.

It is tempting to say with some scholars that
verses 41 and 46 are not in the spirit of Christ's
teaching, but express Jewish ideas which were
unfortunately appropriated by the early Church.
That the verses present a great difficulty to the
modern mind is undoubted, but I am not convinced that we are entitled to cut the knot in this
fashion. If these verses are to go because they
do not fit with the spirit of Christ's teaching, many
others will also have to be excised. The element
of sternness, of denunciation, of drastic judgment
is very deeply engraved in the Gospel portrait of
Jesus whether we like it or not.

Let us examine the verses. In verse 46 the
Authorized Version translates the same Greek word
*aiōnios* by "eternal" and by "everlasting." What
does it mean? What is "everlasting punishment"?

By derivation the word means "belonging" to
the *aion* or age. It does not necessarily mean end-

less, and that is not its primary meaning. "Eternal
life" does not mean ordinary life extended forever
and ever. To prove, as spiritualism claims to do,
that human life goes on beyond the grave, is not
to establish the Christian doctrine of immortality.
Life might be eternal in the chronological sense
and yet far from eternal in the sense of the New
Testament.

The expression "eternal life" occurs forty times
in the New Testament. It is emphatically not
just another phrase for "immortality." In Mark
9. 45-47 and Matthew 7. 14-21 it is used inter-
changeably for "the kingdom of God." In the
Johannine writings it is not too much to say that
eternal life is a summing-up of all the glorious
difference that Christ can make to the man who
accepts Him. It means a fellowship with God
which raises the whole being to a new level of uni-
fied harmonious, effective, Christlike living. "I
am come that they may have *life,* and that they
may have it more abundantly." Eternal life is a
state into which men may enter here and now in
this world. "Time is not a barrier against eternal
life, but the very stuff and means in and by which
we vitally experience and apprehend that life."[4] It
is fundamentally a new kind, a new *quality,* of living. Because of its inherent nature as fellowship
with God, eternal life is endless and endures beyond the grave. But that is a consequence. It is no
definition of the word "eternal" in the New Testament to say it means endless. The Greek word
(*aidios*), that strictly means "eternal" in the sense

[4] Von Hügel, *Eternal Life,* p. 386.

of without beginning or end, is to be found in the New Testament, though only twice. So that we cannot say that the word was not available.

The metaphor of "eternal fire" in verse 41 was apparently drawn from the rubbish dump in the valley of Hinnom (Ge-henna), where the refuse from Jerusalem was cast. It seems that these, like many modern rubbish dumps, were kept alight so that the consumable rubbish might be burned up. These men, we might say, are to be cast on the rubbish heap that the evil may be burned out of them.

Jesus was, of course, not speaking of literal flames. Infinite harm has been done here as elsewhere by interpreting Eastern metaphorical imagery as if it were modern Western scientific prose. This is an illustration of some spiritual process. How far can we press the metaphor? Are they the fires of remorse and repentance when the sinner learns the truth about his own character, the real nature of the deed he has done, and the love of God which he has spurned? Do the fires burn the evil out of him, so that he emerges purified? Even if the flames go on burning, it does not follow that any individual article cast in goes on burning forever. The natural suggestion is that it will be destroyed. Are human beings indestructible? Is the soul naturally immortal or is it only potentially immortal? There is much in the New Testament that might be taken to support that view. No passage in the New Testament explicitly states that *suffering* is endless, though the consequence of sin may be. Annihilation, if that be a fact, would, after all, be a punishment with everlasting consequences, but is not unending torment. Even if we assume that *aiōnios* means "endless," as it sometimes seems to do, it is never found with a word that means suffering.

Is the "punishment" of verse 46 redemptive or merely punitive? The word used here, *kolasis*, comes from the verb to prune, which suggests the removal of the diseased and the superfluous. It is distinguished by Aristotle and Plato as meaning corrective punishment from *timōria*, which means retributive punishment, though it is doubtful if this distinction is recognized in the Septuagint (that is, the Greek Old Testament) or in the New Testament.

I have frankly been asking questions rather than answering them, but they are questions that are raised by the New Testament itself. They ought to be sufficient to curb any easy dogmatism about "eternal punishment," both as to what precisely it means and whether it is incompatible with the spirit of Christ.

It is best to acknowledge frankly that the wisest of us is here out of his depth. We have not sufficient evidence to supply the answers. On the one hand we must not minimize the gravity of the words of Jesus about sin and judgment. The New Testament throughout solemnly insists upon what Baron von Hügel called "abiding consequences." That such words come from the lips of Jesus (as they do, even if we eliminate these particular verses) makes them all the graver. These are not the fulminations of an Amos or a John the Baptist, but the words of the friend of publicans and sinners.

The Judgment is at any rate not arbitrary but based upon fact. We may reject spatial metaphors altogether and insist that heaven and hell are not places but spiritual states. Suppose heaven and hell are the same objectively. To usher the wicked into the unveiled presence of God would be for them torment, though to the good it would be unspeakable joy. "Heaven and Hell," writes Archbishop Temple, "are the two extreme terms of our possible reactions to the gospel of the love of God"[5] (see John 3. 16-21).

On the other hand, there are some Christians who indulge in a kind of spiritual sadism, who gloat over the sufferings of the "damned" and seize upon every word that seems to heighten the torment. Happily, such an attitude is much more rare than it used to be.

In this, as in all such problems, we must base our faith and our judgments upon the character of God revealed in Christ. There are some things that one can say with assurance are out of keeping with the spirit of Christ, and everlasting torment is one of them. It is unthinkable. The great argument that Jesus advanced for immortality was the character of our Father in heaven. If He were in truth the God of Abraham and Isaac and Jacob, how could He let them perish?

We dare not dogmatize, but we can surely hope

---

[5] *Nature, Man, and God,* p. 466.

and trust.   When the Son of man comes in His
glory, it is not merely or even primarily to Judgment.   The consummation of the Kingdom is the
triumph of the love of God.   The "end" comes
because of the love of God, not because of His
wrath.

Love is not sentimentality.   The fires of God
must burn while sin remains.   But can we imagine
—to use the picture from another parable—the God
whom Jesus revealed, as being content with the
fellowship of the ninety and nine while one is still
lost on the hillside?

# INDEX OF GOSPEL PASSAGES

# INDEX